DATE DUE

Permission Slips

Permission Slips

EVERY WOMAN'S GUIDE
TO GIVING HERSELF A BREAK

Sherri Shepherd
WITH LAURIE KILMARTIN

NEW YORK   BOSTON

GRAND CENTRAL
PUBLISHING

Grand Central Publishing

Hachette Book Group

237 Park Avenue

New York, NY 10017

Visit our website at www.HachetteBookGroup.com.

Printed in the United States of America

First Edition: October 2009

10 9 8 7 6 5 4 3 2 1

Grand Central Publishing is a division of Hachette Book Group, Inc. The Grand Central Publishing name and logo is a trademark of Hachette Book Group, Inc.

Library of Congress Cataloging-in-Publication Data

Shepherd, Sherri, 1967–
Permission Slips / Sherri Shepherd.—1st ed.
    p. cm.
  ISBN 978-0-446-54742-0
  1. Shepherd, Sherri, 1967– 2. Television personalities—United States—Biography. 3. Entertainers—United States—Biography. I. Title.
  PN1992.4.S487A3 2009
  791.4502'8092—dc22
  [B]   2009006079

This book is dedicated to my father,

Lawrence A. Shepherd.

You sacrificed your dreams so that I could live mine.

I love you.

Contents

Acknowledgments

So many people I want to thank, so little space.

Everyone who knows me knows how important God is to me, so this is just for Him . . . Thank You, Lord. Throughout this journey, You've always asked the same question: "Do you trust Me?" I just want to say that even though it may seem like I don't, I do. And all those times I fussed and talked back, can we agree that's just water under the bridge? For all those nights You soothed my soul when all I could do was cry, for all You have done, and for the gift of my son. Thank You.

One is only as good as the people she surrounds herself with: The best theatrical agents anyone could have, Mike Eisenstadt and John Frazier. Sixteen years ago, you signed me when nobody knew my name. You believed in me when no one else did. You fought to get me in doors that were shut tight. You encouraged me even when I didn't believe in myself. Pamela Sharp, my publicist, who continued to knock on doors when folks didn't think I could sit on a couch and hold a conversation—you rock, lady! My businesss manager, Bob Bernstein, thank you for being my buffer, helping me get out of debt, and paying my parking tickets so I wouldn't go back to jail.

My literary agent, Yfat Reiss Gendell, from Foundry Literary + Media, I sure appreciate all that you have done to get me this far.

Karen Thomas, my editor, thank you for taking a chance on me. And of course, warm thanks to David Young, Jamie Raab, Emi Battaglia, Les Pockell, Deb Futter, Jennifer Romanello, Evan Boorstyn, Anne Twomey, Diane Luger, Elizabeth Connor, Deborah Feingold, Martha Otis, Karen Torres, Bruce Paonessa, Kelly Leonard, and the invaluable Latoya Smith—thank you so much for your efforts in getting this book to where it is.

Laurie Kilmartin, my co-writer. I cannot say thank you enough for taking my words and my stories and turning them into something so beautiful. You also put into words how crazy I am about God without making me sound too crazy. We're two single mothers who connected on such a level, and I realized after talking to you that I'm not alone. I appreciate your quirky sense of humor. To my extraordinary sisters, Lisa and Lauren. Your strength in day-to-day events inspires me. Lisa, thank you for beating up the girls who picked on me. You have raised five great kids and you'll never have to worry about who's going to take care of you when you're old—who's the smart one? Lori, thank you for the phone calls bugging me to cut Jeffrey's hair and for being the "mama." To my girlfriends who've supported me through the thick and thin of it all: Kim T., Earlene, Dianetta, Cynthia O., Vonda, Yospeha, Angelina, Lydia, Carlease, Christy, Sandy, Lakeitcha, Niecy, and Yvette. A special thanks to Earlene and Niecy, who held my hand through the pain of betrayal. You both gave me a shoulder on which to cry and held the phone for countless hours as I screamed, "Why me?" Every woman needs a male sounding board and Bone, for sixteen years you've been it.

Thanks for being my brother, my friend, and my bodyguard. To my stepmom, Veta, and my sister Jessica. You love my dad, and I love you. To my girls at Ervin, Cohen & Jessup—you supported me and took on my workload so that I could go to my auditions. You stayed up way past your bedtime in order to go to my stand-up gigs. And thank you to Sandy Williams and Barbara Woods for not firing me. It's nice to know that I can always go back to work at the law firm if things don't pan out for me as an author! To Barbara Walters and my wonderful co-hosts at *The View*. You have embraced me and challenged me and make it a joy to come in to work every day. To Jeff Tarpley, the father of my child. Every day I have to say thank you for our son. Who knew that two people could fall in love and produce such a miracle? Jeffrey seems to have gotten the best and filtered out the worst of us. To my son, Jeffrey Charles. What would life be like without hearing your voice and seeing your smile? I first held you and wondered what the heck I'd signed up for. I hold you now and wonder why I waited so long for you. You are my everything, Jeffrey. And lastly this book is dedicated to the millions of women around the world who need a permission slip every day.

And to those family members and friends who I didn't mention by name, please forgive me. You know I love you, but I was told that if I took space for another page, that would come out of my paycheck!

Permission Slips

part one

Doing Everything Wrong

I wish someone would have sat me down when I was a little girl and told me, "Sherri, you can't do anything right."

Hold on—I can explain.

We women are trapped by our circumstances in a way that men are not. We are bound to our families. Our connections to our loved ones are intricate and profound. We stand in the center of a deep pond, surrounded by our children, husbands, boyfriends, parents, siblings, co-workers, and friends. Every move we make has a ripple effect on the people in our pond. If we make a small move, we create a small wave. Big move, big wave. The bottom line is, even if you're doing the right thing, you're making a wave. And that means somebody in your pond is going to get wet.

How many times have you left the house at 8 AM, only to be haunted by competing cries as you shut the door?

"Mommy, I don't want you to go to work!"

"Baby, you gonna put in a few more hours this week so we can pay the cable bill?"

When I say we can't do anything right, I mean that *we can't win*. I'm not implying that men aren't bound to their families, or that their actions don't matter. In fact, men live the same way we do. The only difference is, they don't notice as much if someone gets wet.

That's a huge difference.

Most men lead astonishingly guilt-free lives. I would love to be a man for one day, just so I could enjoy twenty-four hours of not being responsible for anyone else's pain.

My wife's mad at me? Well, she should stop being so emotional.

My dad's disappointed in me? Well, his expectations are too high.

I'm broke? Stupid economy.

That sounds like heaven. But if men don't take enough responsibility, women take on too much. Have you ever sat with your husband at a parent–teacher day-care conference, only to get chewed out by the teacher?

"You need to bring your son to school by 8 AM. When he's late, he misses out on the first art project of the day."

If you're Mom, you're instantly stricken with "bad mother" guilt. But Dad, who thinks he deserves a medal for (a) getting his child to school before noon, and (b) even *being* at the meeting, will get insulted.

"So?"

I envy men. And while I don't believe we women can rewire ourselves to be like them, we must learn to forgive ourselves as much as we forgive others.

Remember: Every time we women make a "right" decision, half the people in our lives will think it's the "wrong" decision. And when they start squawking, we are deluged by guilt. So to feel better, we start judging other women. And that old adage— *When we point our finger, three more are pointing back at us*—proves true, because we save the harshest judgments for ourselves.

I never met a man who obsessed about being a perfect husband, but I know plenty of women who want to be perfect wives.

It ain't happening. We women have to start accepting that no matter what we do, someone's always gonna be cranky about it. Instead of feeling guilty, let's make it okay.

Let's give ourselves *permission* to make ripples in our ponds, even if we get a few people wet. In fact, I recently bought a boxful of pink permission slips, just like we all used to get at school if we had to come in late or leave early. Remember how *free* you'd feel? Leaving the principal's office, running down the hallways with that signed slip . . . it was like having diplomatic immunity (or better yet, *Survivor* immunity). No one could say that you were doing something wrong. Well, I decided to see if they feel as liberating now, with me simply running around my apartment.

And guess what? *They do.* If I'm about to cause a ripple, I pull out my pad and write myself a slip.

"Sherri, you have permission to see a movie with your girlfriend, even though it means you won't have time to read so-and-so's book before she comes on *The View.*"

Then I stick it in a shoe box. If anyone asks what the heck I was doing last night, I have my slip.

The truth is, I'm not even perfect with the slips—in fact, the first one I wrote to myself gave me permission to skip writing a permission slip whenever I wanted.

That way, I'm always covered.

Do you need a slip?

If so, you'd better give yourself one. Immediately. So many facets of our lives conspire to make us feel like crap. If you don't give yourself a break, do you think your kids will? Your husband? Your boss? They want you to keep producing, keep giving. I think you'll see in this book that I've inadvertently made every mistake a woman can possibly make. But I'm not living in a cave, and I haven't quit show business. Instead, I give myself permission to be flawed, and you know what? It's working out okay.

Men

When I look back at my life, I can honestly state that every bout of near insanity can be directly attributed to a man. After I die, I would like to have a sit-down with God, in His family room. The two of us will curl up on a comfy couch, with hot chocolate and M&M's (I'll be able to eat that stuff in Heaven). God will turn on the TV and show me that, lo and behold, my *entire* life has been saved to a DVR. Then He'll hand me the remote and say, "Sherri, ask me anything." I will immediately fast-forward to all my bad dates. And each time a man's about to do something stupid, I will put my life on pause, turn to God, and say, "Lord, what the *heck* is that man thinking?"

Because I need answers.

I admit it, I have a tendency to generalize about men. And that's okay—what are the odds that a man is reading this book? Listen, I'm speaking from my experience, and what I say about men is true for about 80 percent of men in general, and 100 percent of the men I've dated.

Men lead charmed lives. We women always feel like we're not doing enough for the people in our lives. Men are exactly the opposite. The less they do, the happier they are. We are yin, they are yang, and if you ask me, being yang looks like a lot more fun.

When men forget to do something, they don't feel bad for inconveniencing you, they feel bad because they got caught. Have you ever gotten your wires crossed when arranging who's picking up the kids from school? So badly that your kid spent an extra hour outside the building?

Both Mom and Dad feel bad, but for different reasons. Mom, you imagine your child, crying, with no one to play with, wondering when Mommy is going to come. Your heart breaks a little and you feel like a terrible mother. Now let's cut to Dad. He is imagining how mad you're going to be when you find out that he was an hour late. He visualizes that he will not be having sex tonight—or this weekend—if your child is still crying by the time they get home.

After your child is brought home safe and sound, Mom, you will feel guilty for weeks afterward, and probably binge on cheesecake, which will make you feel worse. Dad, on the other hand, will consider the child's safe arrival to be a "crisis solved" and promptly forget the whole thing ever happened.

Charmed lives, I tell you. Charmed. Sometimes I think we overcompensate for their gruffness. For example, on a guilt scale of 1 through 10, if you feel a 5 for leaving your child at school, and he feels a 0, we women will often subconsciously try to make up for our men by working ourselves up to a 10.

Do you know how many binge-cakes a 10 is on the guilt scale? A lot.

My suggestion? Write yourself a permission slip to think like a guy for a day. (Don't worry, you won't be able to do it. But it's fun to try.)

We women also ignore men at our peril. They tell us who they are, but we don't respect their opinion. We think, *Oh, I know that's who you* think *you are, but I know what you* can *be.* As if we're shamans with mystical powers that allow us to change the elements.

Hey, we rationalize, *if Jesus turned water into wine, why can't I change this player into a husband?*

Well, (a) Jesus's feat is considered a miracle, and (b) you ain't Jesus. Women, we need to get realistic about our abilities.

Sometimes men are right, especially when they're telling us who they are.

If you married your husband thinking you would change him, now is the time to give yourself permission to lose that battle. I married a man who *told* me he couldn't be monogamous. *Told* me. Looked me dead in the eye and said monogamy wasn't his thing.

And what did I do? Thank him for dinner and leave the restaurant? No. I decided to *make* him monogamous.

I think you know how that turned out. And if you don't know, hang tight—it will be revealed to you shortly. The bottom line? I failed to change him. And I spent years after my husband cheated feeling like a failure, when the war to make him monogamous was actually unwinnable. Life is hard enough; why do we women want to make it *impossible*?

The next time you are stricken with the female urge to tell a man who he *can* be, after he has told you who he *is*, stop. Stand up. Walk outside. Look up to the clear blue sky, and tell that sky that the only thing keeping it from being bright purple with orange polka dots is a woman's touch. Because that makes about as much sense.

It's painful to reorient your way of thinking. But when you finally see men as they see themselves, your taste in men will change dramatically. It's like you've been going through life slightly buzzed, and now you're sober. And that guy who seemed so cool when you were high? Now you have the clarity to see he's a mess. But that dull civil servant who comes home every night? *Not so bad.*

Write yourself a permission slip to let your man be himself, because that's what he's gonna do anyway.

Of course, there are some men who *do* want you to change them, and it's because they're too lazy to change themselves. Like you, this man wishes he wasn't "water"—and he's hoping you can make good on your promise to turn him into "wine." Now, we have already defined this as a task achievable only by Jesus. But you came along and volunteered to change him—heck, you *prom-*

ised him that you could change him! Home cooking, a white picket fence, a baby . . . you've got it all planned out. So guess who gets blamed when, five years later, he's still "water"?

You.

But now you got a baby to raise.

And as women, if we do divorce (and 50 percent of us do), prepare for judgment and recriminations from every direction, especially if there are kids involved. People will say, "You shoulda tried harder." But if you stay in a bad marriage, someone will say, "You shoulda got a divorce." And if you remarry, you'll get nailed for "caving in too soon." And Lord help you if you stay single, 'cause that means: "You're too picky."

I haven't solved this riddle. Every couple of days, I get a case of the you-shoulda-tried-harders. On Saturday nights, I'm plagued with a case of the you're-too-pickys. Even though I did try hard, and I'm just picky enough.

Women often take on the job of marriage caretaker. If the relationship starts to sour, we're the ones who point it out and insist on therapy. We also find the therapist, make the appointment, and remind our men of the time and day at least twenty times.

Half the time, they forget to show up anyway. Men fix things around the house, but we are charged with fixing the emotional problems. And when the marriage fails, we blame ourselves.

> *If you're divorced, write yourself a permission slip to learn lessons from your "starter" marriage and apply them to your next one.*

Sex

I'm gonna recommend something that might make you want to close this book and throw it across the room.

Celibacy.

Not for wives, of course. In fact, if I could go back in time and have a talk with my married self, the only thing I would whisper in my ear would be, "Put away the vacuum cleaner, and start putting out."

More on that in a second.

I'm a single mom. Obviously I've got no virginity to protect, so it's fair to ask, "What's the point of being celibate now?" Especially since having a toddler kind of makes me celibate by default. As a dater, I'm competing with women who do put out on the first date. In fact, some probably put out *before* the first date. But if a man just wants sex, I'm not the right one, anyway.

I'm no prude. I had lots of sex, and I had it early, too. However, it's been my experience that holding out forces you and your man to work on the emotional and spiritual connection first. And if he's not interested in those things before you have sex, he sure won't be interested in them after.

You don't have to be celibate indefinitely, but it helps separate the wheat from the chaff, and if you're a mom like me, you don't want your kids growing up thinking that "uncles" are men who go away every six months.

And wives? Well, if you've been married for more than five years, congratulations, you know more than me. But if you're a newlywed, please take my advice and have more sex than you feel like having. A quickie can take minutes, and if he's got stamina, it's really just an hour of your life. If you put that never-ending to-do list out of your mind, you might even enjoy it, too. But even if you'd rather be finishing the dishes, take the apron off and give it up. Sex is the glue that can hold you two together when you can't stand each other.

Mark my words, over the course of a fifty-year marriage, you will have moments when you hate each other.

Also sex, like classical music, calms the savage beast, and sometimes that's all men are. If he wants to do something kinky, and it's legal and within your moral comfort zone, try it once. You might like it, and even if you don't, you get points for being a good sport.

We wives get so bogged down in completing chores and taking care of the kids that we forget to take care of the biggest child in the house, our husband. Learn from my mistake. Every so often, let the dishes rot in the sink, put the kids to bed without a bath, shut down your computer, and go get with your man. Chores will always be there, waiting for you, but he might not be.

> *If you're single, write yourself a permission slip to wait until you're ready. If you're married, put away your permission slips, put on a black slip, and finish this book tomorrow.*
>
> *What are you still doing here? Go!*

Mom

Going from wife to mother is a game changer. (Or girlfriend to mother. Or one-night stand to mother. No judgments here; things happen.)

We moms are backed into a corner. We want the best for our babies, and there's no end to things you can do to make your child smarter, healthier, happier, and more successful. Here are just a few things that can freak you out during your pregnancy: mercury in tuna, hormones in the water, Baby Einstein—yes or no? Plastic bottles or glass ones? What causes autism, ADD, ADHD, and asthma? How come pregnant women in Europe get to drink wine every day but I can only drink it once a week?

Fifty Web sites will give you fifty different answers. It's not enough that you sacrifice your body and your life, now you gotta get an advanced degree in biology—while you're throwing up.

And the kid ain't even born yet.

> *Before you forget, write yourself a permission slip to give the baby tap water, from a plastic bottle.*

When we become moms, we become more responsible. When men become dads, they stay the same, which means they actually become less responsible.

For example, let's say no one does the laundry for a week. At the last minute, your son has to wear dirty underwear to school.

You feel like a bad mother. But your husband? He thinks it's funny, and he'll convince your son it's funny, too. Men have a lower threshold for what's disgusting. So if the laundry piles up, guess who's doing it at 2 AM? The parent who doesn't think it's hilarious to wear filthy underpants—you.

> ***Write yourself a permission slip to wash only your and your child's laundry. If your husband thinks it's so funny to wear dirty briefs, let him.***

And the worst insult is that no matter how great a mom you are, at some point your children will hate you. They will even hate the good things you did. In fact, when your child becomes a teenager, all the good things you did as a parent will be used against you.

Are you a stay-at-home mom?

"Mom, you were a terrible role model! I'm never going to be like you!"

Are you a working mom?

"Mom, you put your career first!"

Do you work two jobs so your kid can go to private school?

"Mom, you were never home when I needed you!"

Did you quit your second job so you could be home when your child needed you?

"Mom, I had to go to public school!"

You can't win. My son is only three, but I'm taking as much video as possible. In ten years, I want to be able to look back and remind myself that, at one time, he was adorable, and he liked me.

> *Write yourself another slip: When it comes to your children, you have permission to do everything wrong. Because according to them, you did anyway.*

Family

It takes having kids before you realize that maybe your parents weren't all that bad, crazy, ridiculous, or lame. How many times did your parents tell you, "Wait until you have kids!" Of course, you'd smugly vow to be so much better, cooler, funnier, funner, or nicer than they were. Cut to twenty years later—you're saying the exact same things to your kid that your mom said to you.

Are there any relationships more complex than the ones we have with our parents? I was barely twenty-three when my mom passed away. We fought like cats and dogs (or I should say "mothers and daughters") for most of my teens. Luckily, we made up before she died. My dad and I are very close, although he lives in Chicago, so I see him infrequently.

Parents are frustrating because you can't change them. Of course, you can't change *anyone*, but at least with men there is the *illusion* that you can change them. (As we discussed, you will learn the bitter truth at some point.) And your kids—well, you're convinced you can direct them.

But the parents? No matter how old you are, one of them

will always give you that look of disapproval, the look that says: *I wanted more for you.* Unfortunately, you can't change their expectations. If they wanted you to stay in a nine-to-five and you quit to join the Peace Corps, they will be disappointed. If they wanted you to get married and you got a divorce, they will be disappointed. If they wanted you to be a Jehovah's Witness and you became a Pentecostal, guess what—you let them down.

It's okay to do that, because usually you're right. My dad was disappointed when I quit my nine-to-five. I wanted a storybook ending to my life, and he thought that was impractical. In fact, he'd had so many part-time jobs that he thought my job at the legal firm, with its pension and 401(k), *was* a storybook ending.

I disagreed. After many years, my handsome prince came in the form of *The View*, but if that hadn't happened, he'd probably still be giving me that *I-told-you-not-to-quit-a-solid-job* look.

Parents come around to your way of thinking once you have success. If I was still temping and taking the bus to auditions, my dad would not be happy for me.

I think I understand my mom a lot more now that I have hopes and dreams for my son. Our fights were about my rebellion. She saw that I was in pain and thought the church could take it away. I saw different, and my journey took me down a few paths she wasn't thrilled with. I'm pretty sure that she would be proud of me now, and I know she would be crazy about her grandson. A great freedom comes from making peace with your parents.

And it's ultimately a compliment to them when you declare your independence from their expectations. It's like you're telling them, "You raised a person who thinks for herself and congratulations, because I'm finally gonna do what I want!"

> ***So write yourself a permission slip
> to disappoint your parents a little bit.
> You never know when they might come
> around.***

Thighs

Can we women all just let up on our thighs? As you'll soon find out, I grew up around amputees. In my neighborhood, *somebody* was always losing *something* to diabetes. A toe, a foot, a leg. To me, knowing someone with one leg was as American as baseball and syrup on apple pie. (And if you've never put syrup on apple pie, then your family members probably have all their legs.) I don't care how thick your ankles are, if you've got both of 'em, you're doing better than a lot of folks.

Trying to have a perfect body is a lose–lose. From what I can tell, no matter how many pounds you lose, you could always lose five more. There's always another pair of jeans you can't quite zip, always one more celebrity who bounced back from pregnancy better than you did. (Nicole Kidman, anyone?)

Once you head down that path of body obsession, it's near impossible to veer off. You're either bingeing, purging, starving, or exercising. Counting calories like Bridget Jones, hating yourself for eating something good. Feeling guilty, eating more. And repeat. How many times have you canceled a date or something fun because you "felt fat"? And you probably weighed exactly the same as you did the day before. But you ate too much and now you don't want to look anyone in the eye.

Stop me when I've described your life.

Diabetes helped me veer off that path. When I stopped dieting for vanity and started dieting to stay alive, my perspective changed. Every day my blood sugar is stable is a good day. That's twenty-four more hours of love to give my son. My weight still fluctuates—I wish it didn't. But I see the big picture, and so far I'm still in it, hanging out with my little man. We're having a good time. And if I can keep my emotions on an even keel, it's not too hard to eat normally. I try to avoid getting too lonely, hungry, tired, or mad. A binge could really knock me out of that perfect picture.

It's ironic—I missed so many fun times because I didn't feel good about my body. And now that I feel good about my body, I'm too tired to have fun! Don't let this happen to you.

> *In other words, write yourself a slip to eat something, so that you don't feel deprived and eat everything. If I'm too late and you just ate everything, backdate yourself an all-access pass to the pantry and start over tomorrow.*

Aging

If we're lucky enough to stay in the picture, then we're gonna get old. Every damn one of us. Not even the big shots can stave off aging forever. I had an epiphany when I was reading a gossip magazine. Apparently, during Madonna's divorce, Guy Ritchie said that making love to her was like "curling up with a piece of gristle."

Whoa.

Now, Madonna was fifty years old at the time, and working out about four hours a day. She was in amazing shape, better shape than most of us are, *ever*, in our entire lives. She had the best plastic surgeons and dermatologists at her disposal, and still, her younger husband called her "a piece of gristle." That tells me that none of us is safe. You fall apart, you're a fat cow. You keep it together, you're gristle.

Give me a break.

If we women took the hours we waste worrying about our looks and used them to find a cure for cancer, in five years Lance Armstrong could stop wearing bracelets. Our looks are an obsession that starts in our teens and never quite goes away. Aging follows the same trajectory for everyone—for a while you look "great," then you look "good." Next you look "good for your age," then you're "hanging in there," and finally you're dead. No quotation marks, you're actually dead. If you find a way around that time line, bottle it and sell me some.

We're all "too" something. Too fat, thin, light, dark, tall, short, old—every adjective under the sun except *young*. In our culture, no one's too young. Which is great when you're twenty-five. The world revolves around your natural collagen and fast metabolism. After you pass thirty, you notice that you aren't being catered to as much. At forty, there is a definitive shift.

Remember that scene in *It's a Wonderful Life* where an old guy says to Jimmy Stewart, "Youth is wasted on the young"? It's true. (By the way, you know you're old when that line makes you laugh. I never met a teenager who thought that line was funny.)

Imagine if the twenty-year-old you possessed the wisdom

of your forty-year-old self. You'd have realistic dreams and the confidence to pull them off. And what if the forty-year-old you had the audacity of your twenty-year-old self? All right, I'm getting confused here, too, but my point is, I agree with that old man. The only time youth and old age cross paths is when our ninety-year-old body has a one-year-old's bladder.

I see my girlfriends and me wasting a lot of time. Whether we're sixteen or forty, we're always trying to look thirty. We have to stop that before we turn into "cool moms." You've seen those women—they can't quite accept that they've moved on to another stage in their lives. They wear their daughters' jeans, they shop at Forever 21 (for themselves), and their foreheads don't move. It's weird. Sometimes I want to lean over and whisper in their ears, "I know you're the same age as me. *I know it.*"

You can't Botox away the look in your eye that says, *Honey, I've seen it all.*

And why would you want to? All the fun women have been around the block. They're the ones with stories to tell. They've made mistakes that will make your jaw drop and make you feel like you're not the only klutz in town. In fact, I don't want to sit next to you at a dinner party unless (a) your heart's been broken, or (b) you've been in jail. And if your heart was broken *while* you were in jail, I won't leave your side.

Can we women, as a group, agree to get old and ugly together? Let's have crow's-feet, flappy underarm skin, and that deep, vertical frown line between our eyebrows. We can show our daughters what they're supposed to look like when they get old. (And give our sons realistic expectations of their wives.) C'mon, I don't want to have surgery so I can keep up with y'all. I don't like scalpels.

> *So write yourself a permission slip to look your age. And if you're Madonna, write yourself a slip to skip Pilates today.*

Girlfriends

Sometimes we women take our girlfriends for granted. We call them when we're lonely, and drop them when we're not. We find love, fall down the "man-hole," and completely disappear . . . until we're single again. C'mon. That's no way to maintain a lifelong relationship.

My circle of friends has saved or changed my life too many times to count. And that circle is always contracting and expanding. I lost some friends to religious differences (theirs, not mine) and gained others as motherhood and *The View* took me to new places, figuratively and literally. But over my lifetime, my girlfriends have given me a stability I couldn't find in my relationships or, sometimes, even in my own family. They encouraged me to try stand-up comedy, covered for me when I was late for work, told me when it was time to leave a no-good man. (Okay, *men*. There was more than one.) They prayed for me and then reminded me I could pray, too.

Often, we get so caught up in the impossible task of doing everything "right" that we forget to reconnect with our roots. Our base. Strength can be found in comfort, and sometimes all you need is a familiar voice to say, "Girl, I hear you."

> *Sound familiar? If so, then write yourself a permission slip to call an old friend and pick up where you left off.*

Faith

Oh, hey, speaking of old friends, I should probably add God to that list. Atheists, feel free to roll your eyes and skip ahead a few pages. Just understand that I'm not preaching, I'm sharing. And if you think I'm a lunatic, that's okay. I would be honored to be your goofy, lunatic friend.

I know many people who were, like me, raised in a strict religion. And if, as an adult, you resist adhering to the strict rules you were raised with as a child, it's important to remember that you can have your own relationship with God. You don't need to go through a church elder, a pastor, a minister, or a priest to pray. Lots of people rebel against their church. How many ex-Catholics, Mormons, Baptists, and Witnesses do you know? Some of us stray so "far" that we think we are unreachable, that we can't return to God. You might be reading this thinking, *Well, that's fine for you, Sherri, but I've had abortions and promiscuous sex; I've hurt people I love.*

All I have to say to you is, "Ditto."

I'm living proof that at any point in your rebellion, you can drop to your knees, close your eyes, clasp your hands together, and say, "Hi."

You will not get yelled at or told to sit in a corner. You will be welcomed back like the prodigal son, and if your homecoming is anything like mine, you will wonder why you ever left.

It has been my experience that God just wants you back. Remember running away from home when you were a kid? When you returned, the first thing your mom did was hug you and cry. The second thing she did was grab a wooden spoon, bend you over her knee, and swat you hard on the behind, yelling, "Don't you *ever* run away again."

Coming home to God is like that, minus the punishment— because you're already doing that to yourself. We are rarely having real fun during those "away" spells. I believe that God doesn't pull out the wooden spoon upon our return because being away from Him is enough of a swat on the behind. He just hugs us and cries with delight.

I truly don't know how atheists do it—they must have stronger constitutions than I do, because the times I've been without God have been the loneliest times in my life. And all that pain was self-inflicted. I could've made the call at any time, I just didn't think God would want to hear from me after all the things I'd done.

Boy, was I wrong.

When I ended a rough patch in my thirties with a loud wail to Heaven, the response on the other end of the line was so joyous, it was almost embarrassing.

"SHERRI! Where you been? I HAVE MISSED YOU!"

I tried to explain I'd been out doing this and that, dating felons, serving time for warrants. God cut me off.

"I know! I'm just so thrilled you're back. You were always My favorite!"

Of course He says that to everyone, but still, it's nice to hear. No matter how long you've been gone, no matter what you've done, you're always welcome back to God's house. I believe that certain embrace is the gift of faith, and if I can give that gift to my son, I will have done my job. We humans will always stray, always. The story of Adam and Eve, whether you believe it actually happened or not, is the perfect example of how we humans will fail at almost every opportunity. But the amazing thing is that the path back to God is always lit, always safe, and always open. Like Motel 6, God always leaves a light on for you.

I hope my son knows that when he runs away God will take him back, no questions asked. I also hope he knows that I'll bend him over my knee and swat his behind with a wooden spoon. Because I'm human that way.

> *So write yourself a permission slip to come back to God at any time. In fact, if you kneel while you scribble, you're halfway there.*

My fellow Americans

I wasn't raised in a politically active family, and look at me now. Maybe it's the homework I do to prepare for *The View*, or Barack Obama's presidency, or the fact that I have a personal stake in the future (my son), but politics has become a very interesting subject to me.

I'm proof that you don't need a master's in political science to have an informed opinion. Start small. Follow an issue that has a direct effect on your life and you'll probably find yourself tracking the moves of the secretary of state in a few months. The other ladies of *The View* were miles ahead of me when I started, and I'm having fun catching up.

If you're starting from scratch, like I did, I have some advice: First, don't be afraid to ask questions, and if someone tries to make you feel dumb, start talking to someone who doesn't. Anyone who would belittle you for trying to get smarter is a jerk, and you can quote me on that.

Looking dumb is an understandable fear. All I can say is take comfort in the fact that no one has ever looked dumber than I did when I said I wasn't sure if the earth is round. On national television, and then YouTube, about ten million times (so far). Just know that you will never feel as intellectually humiliated as I did during the weeks after I made that unfortunate statement.

In fact, feel free to use me as a worst-case scenario to make yourself feel better. No matter how lost you feel when it comes to understanding politics or global warming or the deficit, at least you know the shape of our planet!

The more interested I've become in issues, the more engaged I've become as a citizen. I've been privileged enough to meet ordinary women from other countries during my time at *The View,* and hearing about their lives has made me so grateful I was born in the United States. Like my faith, I want to pass on that gratitude to my son, and to the people I meet every day.

We take when we're young. We take energy, attention, love. When we get older, we are able to return the favor. Not just to our families but also to our neighbors, our communities, and our country. Do something tiny. Help clean up a park or walk a shelter dog. If you can do it with your kids, even better. I've learned that a political view doesn't make you patriotic, but the acts of participating and giving back sure do.

> *Write yourself a permission slip to bloom where you're planted and start small.*

I've made every mistake that a decent person can make, and I'm still here, still learning. Probably like you, I could have given up about a million times by now, but I didn't. Hopefully, I've got at least forty more years' worth of gaffes and mistakes to make. I can't wait!

One thing I've learned while writing this book is that I'm the Fairy Godmother of people who wish they could have a do-over. If I had a wand, I would grant you that wish.

part two

Permission to Date, Love, Marry, and Divorce the Wrong Guy

I've dated more losers than you have. It's a fact. Don't even try to top me. I don't care how many wrong-man stories you've got, I've got one more, and it's twice as bad. You got cheated on? Well, so did I, but I got cheated on when I was *pregnant.* So did you? Well, I was on bed rest. So were you? Well, I went through months of IVF treatments to get pregnant. You too? Well, the girl he slept with was fifteen years younger than me. Oh, you're *still* nodding your head? Well, get ready to surrender, because that girl—who was fifteen years younger than me—*also* got pregnant.

Hello? You still there? No? You're finally waving a white flag. Shoot, I win again. And listen—I'm not bragging. If loser-loving was an Olympic event, I would be Michael Phelps. And that reminds me—if I ever dated Michael Phelps, he would probably cheat on me, too. Now pop some corn, pour yourself a glass of wine, and thank the Good Lord you ain't me. 'Cause this chapter's just starting.

The at-least girl

How did I turn into the at-least girl? You know the at-least girl—she's the one who makes you say, "At least my man ain't doing that."

I blame my diary. Every day, I wrote down each teenage feeling I had. Love, lust, fear, and obsession. I wrote down the things I did and things I wish I hadn't. My diary was my best friend. My diary didn't judge me and it always greeted me with a fresh, clean page. My diary was like a dog that didn't need to be walked. And I was a teenager in the 1980s, when feelings were secret and shameful. We didn't call them "journals," and we sure as heck didn't blog. My diary came with a metal lock and a key, and I secured that little book every time I closed it. I hid my diary in the garage, where it was safe from the prying eyes of my little sister Lisa.

Or so I thought.

Lisa came to me one day with a smile on her face and some paper in her hand. And not just paper, but pages. Pages ripped from my diary, which she found in the garage. The lock that I'd trusted with my heart had apparently popped open with a bobby pin.

"I'm telling Mama," she said.

"Please don't," I begged, "please!"

Lisa had seized just three pages from my diary, but they were the pages that would sink my battleship. Those three pages were to the rest of my teenage years what that blue dress from the Gap would be to Bill Clinton's presidency—undeniable proof of illicit sexual activity. Those pages detailed the joy and pain of losing my virginity—at age fourteen. Whether she was jealous or just mean, I don't know, but my sister Lisa, all of twelve years old, marched up to our mother and gave her the evidence.

Now, I'm not a theologian, but I'm gonna guess that most religions frown at the idea of fourteen-year-old girls having sex. But I'd be surprised if any religion frowned as hard or as long as the Jehovah's Witnesses. After she finished reading, my mother called a church elder. Our congregation had three elders; they were old men, two black and one white. The elders instructed us to meet them immediately at the Kingdom Hall. My mom, my dad, and I got in the car. My dad didn't know why we'd been summoned, but he knew it wasn't good.

"Tell your father what you did," my mother said from the front seat. "Tell your father."

I did. It was, at that time, the most humiliating moment of my life. (Of course, I didn't know that dozens of more humiliating moments were lined up around the corner, waiting to take a whack at me.)

The three of us sat down with the elders and talked. Well, I talked. Everyone else listened, with their eyes closed. Occasionally, a head would shake. The elders, in front of my parents, asked me intimate and direct questions about my first sexual experience.

"What did that boy do to you?"

"Did he put his fingers inside you?"

I wanted to demand the return of my pages so I could reread my notes. I don't remember everything they asked, but I bet those three old wise men got their jollies watching a fourteen-year-old girl talk about sex. Their final question left me stumped.

"Did you have oral sex?"

I didn't even know what oral sex was, but that old church elder was so disgusted when he said it, I was convinced that not only did I *have* oral sex, but I probably enjoyed it, too.

Virginity: Better kept than lost

Looking back, that night of evil was much more innocent than the church elders imagined. Of course, sex at age fourteen is not good. But also, sex at age fourteen is *literally* not good. Two teenagers bumping uglies and checking for grown-ups every thirty seconds isn't the makings of a great night. And it's not like right after my cherry was popped, I was chomping at the bit, "Damn, I gotta have me some of that, *every day!*"

In fact—and this is not a critique of Gilbert (more on him in a moment)—my first time was a letdown. Because from the moment I got my first period, all I heard from my parents and the church was how special my virginity was. A *gift*. Something to be given to my husband, whom I would marry at the Kingdom Hall.

My parents weren't the only ones obsessed with my virginity. My friends at school thought on it, too, but they looked on virginity as a problem that needed a solution. A booger to be flicked off the end of my finger, preferably before sophomore year. It was explained to me that people who had sex were always screaming and hollering because they were so happy. Well, who wouldn't want some of that, every day?

"Sex," one girlfriend insisted, "is awesome." That was all I needed, I was sold. All that was missing was the right guy to deflower this impatient virgin.

One day, my girlfriend Rhonda and I were hanging out at the pool at her apartment complex. By the way, this is already a recipe for disaster. If I ever have a daughter, there will be no hanging out at apartment complexes, and no hanging out at pools. And don't get me started on apartment complexes with pools.

Oh, let me tell you about Rhonda

Rhonda was my best friend growing up. We were like peanut butter and jelly, Batman and Robin. (I was Robin.) Rhonda had a butt, hips, and breasts. All I had were teeth. No hips, no boobs—just oodles of eager buck teeth. In fact, we both resembled members of the Jackson Family. Rhonda looked like Janet, and I looked like Michael—when he was four. The boys loved Rhonda and tolerated me. I didn't resent Rhonda, I worshipped her. And I was honored to hold her purse when she needed to go make out with someone.

Every year, the Witnesses have an Assembly at a huge arena. Twenty-five thousand Witnesses, studying the Bible from 8 AM to 5 PM. One year, Rhonda and I attended together. During the two-hour lunch breaks, we went boy-hunting. Actually, I would spot them, and she would go in for the kill.

During one break, she met a boy named Robert. Rhonda and Robert. When your names sound that cute together, you *have* to go to second base. We snuck out to Robert's parents' car. Yes, *we.* I was there, too. And not for a threesome. Nope, I was there to watch. R and R French-kissed in the front seat, while ol' SS here watched from the backseat. I was like a Red Cross monitor, just making sure no one's rights were violated. What a show. I wished I'd had a box of Lemonheads and a Coke to go with it. Rhonda had some good moves, and Robert wasn't too shabby, either.

I was so fascinated with the romantic matinee playing up front that I forgot to keep my eyes peeled for grown-ups. A church elder knocked on the window.

"What's going on in there?" He'd been patrolling the parking lot for lust.

"Nothing, talking," I said. In addition to holding Rhonda's purse, I was also responsible for alibis.

"Get out of that car. Now."

We got in trouble, of course, but it was too late for me. While this little genie was not out of her bottle yet, she sure was tired of watching life from inside it.

A green-eyed Puerto Rican named Gilbert

Gilbert Hernandez was a green-eyed Puerto Rican who made my body wiggle a little inside. He was also hanging out at Rhonda's apartment complex that day. Now, I was not in love with Gilbert, and I had no thoughts of becoming his wife or even his girlfriend. But I did want to start screaming and hollering as soon as possible. To me, Gilbert Hernandez was up to the task. Just like that, I decided, *I'm gonna give it up to him.*

Maybe I should've flirted a little, or at least made him buy me a milk shake, but even at fourteen I was a busy lady with no time to waste.

"Gilbert," I said to him, splashing myself a little, "Gilbert, I want to give you my virginity."

"Okay," he said, like this had happened yesterday, too.

It was a very simple transaction. If we'd been a little more savvy, we would've shaken hands and had our respective secretaries set up a meeting for Gilbert to receive my gift.

That night at Rhonda's, we were getting ready for bed. Oh, that's another recipe for my disaster cookbook: *sleepovers* at an apartment complex with a pool. Bad idea. Rhonda and I were in our pajamas, talking about girls we hated, girls we liked, and marrying Michael Jackson, when we heard rocks hit Rhonda's second-floor window.

It was Gilbert, who'd come to claim what was rightfully his. He brought his cousin, who was probably praying that Rhonda needed a hand with her virginity. They wanted to come up. Rhonda's mom was down the hall, in the living room. Now, there's not much I won't say, but even I couldn't say, "Mrs. Johnson, can Gilbert come in? He's supposed to have sex with me tonight. Oh, and his cousin's here, too, in case your daughter wants some."

We did what any teenager who's been to the movies would do in that situation. We unfurled a bedsheet from the window. Gilbert tried to climb up it and fell. It turned out that fashioning a bedsheet into a rope that can support two horny boys was a special effect beyond our capabilities. There was, however, a tree near Rhonda's window. Gilbert and his cousin climbed it. Somehow they were able to Spider-Man-swing themselves toward the window and fall in. I wish I'd taken note that night—men will risk breaking their necks if they believe they have a shot at getting laid.

Once Gilbert landed, I had no idea what to do. I didn't want to just dive into the sex right away. After all, Gilbert would also be my first kiss. He didn't say anything, so I took control.

"Aren't we supposed to kiss?" I asked.

"Sure we can do that, too," he said, shrugging. Gilbert was easygoing, I'll give him that.

We kissed, and then we started fooling around. After the five-minute mark, I decided my girlfriends had lied. There was no screaming and hollering—just grunting and breathing.

Then, at the six-minute mark, I realized that my girlfriends had sort of told the truth. Yes, I *was* screaming and hollering, but not because I was happy. I was screaming because sex hurt and I was hollering because I wanted it to feel good. Of course, Gilbert couldn't tell the difference and thought we were both having a great time.

The next day, I had terrible diarrhea. I don't know if that was just my nervous stomach or a punishment from God (or

Montezuma). But we were all supposed to go to Great America amusement park and I bailed. It was my first day of being a nonvirgin and I was experiencing sore thighs and unpredictable backside explosions and I just needed to stay home and deal with that.

I never saw Gilbert again. (We didn't go to the same school.) I wonder if he recognizes me on TV. Does he poke his wife in the ribs and say, "That's Sherri Shepherd, I was her first"? I'd like to look him up, just so I could ask him if his other conquests got diarrhea the day after. I tried Googling him, but Gilbert Hernandez is a surprisingly common name. I should've lost my virginity to an "Adolf" or something.

> *Write yourself a permission slip to have a disappointing first-time story. If we all started admitting that losing our virginity sucked, maybe our daughters will postpone their first time for a couple extra years.*

Put on reproof

When you're a Jehovah's Witness, once you've committed a sin, the elders put you on something called "reproof." There are two kinds of reproof—public and private. Public reproof is about as awful as it sounds. On Sunday morning, in front of the entire congregation, the elders announce that you're being reproved for a sin. They don't tell anyone what the sin is—which makes it worse, because people just start guessing. In the case of a fourteen-year-old girl, your sin is pretty obvious. You had sex. About a year or so later, Rhonda would be sentenced to public reproof. (Even if the church elders had wanted to give her private reproof, they couldn't, because she'd gotten pregnant.)

While you're on public reproof, no one in the congregation is allowed to talk to you for three months. And when you're a Jehovah's Witness, you don't associate with many people outside the church, so that means no one *in your world* is allowed to talk to you for three months. The intention is to make you feel so alone and isolated that you'll never commit that sin again. Once the three months are up, it's as if nothing ever happened. You are welcomed back to the fold. I believe this is a way to make Witnesses emotionally dependent on the church, and in many cases it works. In fact, Rhonda is still a Witness.

I was terrified of public reproof. When it was my turn to meet with those elders, I did what men accuse women of doing every time they want to get out of something. I cried. Actually, I wailed. A full-on biblical wailing that would melt the heart of an Old Testament pharaoh.

"I'm sorry!" I screamed.

"I'll never do it again!" I hollered.

It worked. I got private reproof. No one in the congregation would ever know what I'd done. Of course, private reproof still comes with a punishment. I was forbidden to talk to any boys. No talking, no flirting, no sly glances, no nothing, unless it was absolutely necessary for schoolwork.

I promised to live up to my end of the bargain, but I had doubts. I was boy-crazy and part of me was thinking, *Yeah, the first time wasn't so great, but the second time might just be my charm.* Even then, I was always looking on the bright side.

> *Write yourself a permission slip to*
> *scream and holler if you must. If it got*
> *me out of public reproof, it'll get you out*
> *of a speeding ticket.*

Go west, young woman!

We moved to California when I was seventeen. But even that didn't get me off the Witnesses' radar. The church elders in Chicago sent a letter to the Kingdom Hall in Los Angeles, instructing them that their newest parishioner, Sherri Shepherd, was not to communicate with any boys. Ever.

Most teenagers would hate moving across the country. You have to make new friends at a new school and you have no say in the matter. Well, almost as soon as we landed, I knew Los Angeles and I were going to get along just fine. For one reason: The Shepherd family would be attending the same Kingdom Hall as another Jehovah's Witness you may have heard of—Michael Jackson.

The thought of MJ today probably makes you roll your eyes or hide your children. So I'm gonna ask you to go to the garage and open up that box where you keep those round black disks with holes in them. Records, I think they're called. Pull one out called *Off the Wall*. Go ahead and look at it. Michael Jackson, leaning back in all his glory, looking black and beautiful. Flip through a few more until you find *Thriller*. Those lined eyes, those little curls. I can't vouch for the post-*Thriller* MJ, but back then Michael Jackson was the man.

And he went to my church.

I knew where he lived, and I used to take the bus from the ghetto part of the Valley where we lived, Van Nuys, to the cool part of the Valley where he lived, Encino. I would wait outside his gate, and every time a limo with darkened windows pulled out, I'd shout, "I LOVE YOU, MICHAEL JACKSON." I couldn't figure out who I was shouting it to—probably Tito.

I never saw Michael, but occasionally I'd see Janet and LaToya at Bible study. For the record, I believe Janet flashed her nipple during the Super Bowl on purpose, and as a former Witness, it made sense to me.

My California high school years weren't wild. I had a few crushes. A boy named Gary Owens gave me my first French kiss, which sounds more exotic in theory than it is in practice. But dating was seen by my parents and my church as a prelude to marriage. And, no offense to Gary Owens, but I don't think we would have lasted. What I loved most about high school in L.A. was that I found a new crew of girlfriends to hang out with. And those girls grew into the women that I'm still friends with today.

His name was Terry

It wasn't until after high school that I had my first serious boyfriend. I was eighteen or nineteen, studying for my legal secretary degree. He was a Bad Boy—capital B, capital B. Every religious girl has one, and mine was named Terry.

Terry was ten years older than me. Terry rode a motorcyle. Terry picked me up from school on his motorcycle.

Heaven.

I don't know what Terry saw in me, except that I was easy to please. I had no experience with boyfriends, so I had no expectations of Terry. In fact, a boyfriend with a motorcycle exceeded *all* my expectations, so anything else Terry did was gravy. *Terry, you're paying for dinner? Cool! At McDonald's? Neat! And you had my fries supersized? I LOVE YOU.*

So naive was I that anything Terry wanted me to do, I did. Without question. He called me one night before a date.

"Sherri, tonight I want you to wear all black."

"Okay! Why?"

"It's a surprise."

He picked me up at my mom's, and we drove into the Hollywood Hills. Above Franklin, into the canyons. Where beautiful big houses are perched on the hillside. The kind of house you look at when you're poor and think, *Someday I'm gonna live in a house like that.*

Terry parked the motorcycle. "Sherri, we're going on an adventure."

"What is it?!" I asked, excited.

"Let's just walk," he said.

Walk? Something didn't feel right. *We're both dressed in black, and now he wants us to walk on the side of a dark, winding road?*

"We're gonna get hit by a car," I said. We headed toward the bushes and came upon a beautiful home, with stairs leading up to a deck.

"Sherri, I dare you to walk up those steps."

I got a creepy feeling. This was not a fun game, and I suddenly realized that I was not a fan of surprises. But he kept goading me, and he was still "cool." I walked up a few steps.

"See how far up those stairs you can go," he whispered from below.

"Terry, I can see the lady doing her dishes through her window!"

I guess she could see me, too, because a police car came

around. Terry pulled me into the bushes. I had a bad feeling, I wanted to go home. Why did he want me dressed in black, climbing up people's steps like a cat burglar?

"I'm going home," I said.

I whispered a private good-bye to his motorcycle and walked until I found a bus stop. I got myself home the old-fashioned way. Public transportation. Years later, I realized he was planning to rob that lady's house, and I was there to play the part of the unwitting accomplice. Some date. As soon as this dawned on me, I fell on my knees and thanked God for protecting stupid people.

You're probably thinking, *Good thing you broke up with Terry that night.*

I stayed with him for a few more years. Look, I'm loyal. I will stay with you through McDonald's dinners and home-invasion scouting. I will stay even if you just disappear for weeks at a time. After all, I'm young. And naive. And in love. And let's not forget, you have a motorcycle.

One night I was watching the evening news with my dad. The lead story was about a recent fire. Apparently the cops had a suspect.

"Sherri," my dad asked, "is that Terry on the news?"

Sure enough, there on the TV, perp-walking with the flair of a ballroom dancer, was my boyfriend, Terry. That was the last time I saw him—with his head being pushed into the back of a police cruiser. My ex-boyfriend, the arsonist.

> *Write yourself a permission slip*
> *to leave any man who takes you to a*
> *McDonald's on your first date. Like*
> *sex, fast-food dates should be saved for*
> *marriage.*

Learning to spot red flags

When it came to men, I did not pick up on obvious warning signs. It never would have occurred to me that Terry was an arsonist. If he'd been reading *Fire-Starting for Dummies*, I would have thought, *Wow, he has so many interests—Terry is a Renaissance Man!*

I cringe when I think of all the dumb situations I put myself in. Once I had a blind double date with a friend and her boyfriend. The four of us met at her boyfriend's house, and, during our casual conversation, I noticed that his house was littered with guns. A machine gun on the dining room table, a handgun in a fruit bowl, a "Glock" (I think) on top of the microwave, another one by a photo of Mom.

"What does your boyfriend do?" I asked my friend.

"Oh, he's a drug dealer."

I should have faked a headache and left. I didn't, because "drug dealer" sounded like a profession. After all, people do drugs, and it makes sense that an industry exists to serve their needs. I knew drug dealing was illegal, but everything in Los Angeles seems illegal. So instead of leaving, I cheerfully said, "Drug dealing, that's cool! What does that entail?"

Yup, that was me. Making polite chitchat about someone's career, like the boyfriend was an insurance salesman. I could have been shot in a drive-by, shot by the boyfriend, shot accidentally, or just busted for possession. When I hear about young girls getting tangled up in their boyfriends' crimes, I really have compassion for them. When I see them on *Jerry Springer*, live via satellite from a women's prison, saying, "I didn't realize, I didn't know," I believe them. Naïveté plus love often equals something bad—crime, an unintended pregnancy. You aren't thinking about the ramifications of your actions. You just hope the end result doesn't ruin your life, or anyone else's.

I'm lucky. God never let me mess up so badly that I couldn't come back from it. He definitely keeps me around so I can keep screwing up. Half the souls in Heaven must pull up a chair when I'm about to screw up. "Hey, y'all, check it out. Sherri's at the grocery store and she just wrote a bad check!"

I dated a few other bad boys (lowercase b, lowercase b). And even now, they still manage to track me down and ask for a favor. One wanted money. I said no. Another asked me to play his music on the Daytime Emmys. I said no. Another said he would release naughty pictures to the press. I said, *Please do.* I remember those pictures. I was in my twenties and I looked amazing. I had one chin and no wrinkles. In fact, I asked him to send the pictures to me so I could release them myself. He had no connections and would probably go the *National Enquirer* route, but I could ask Barbara to call *Vanity Fair.*

> *Write yourself a permission slip to leave when you are in over your head. If it seems illegal to you, it probably is illegal to the police.*

Finally, a "good guy"

My bad-boy run ended with a man named Charlie. I decided it was time for someone more responsible, and Charlie was a teacher. By this time, I was doing stand-up comedy, and we met at one of my gigs. Note to self (and any comedians reading this): Never date anyone who's seen you onstage. People confuse the stage-you with the real-you. And in most cases, the reason you created a stage-you in the first place was to offset the pain of being the real-you. Charlie was attracted to my spontaneous side. He liked that I was different, that I was social and had lots of friends.

It took poor Charlie two years to realize that I wasn't right for him. That "different" meant irresponsible, that "spontaneous" meant I do everything last-minute. And being "social" meant I was going to cheat on him, probably with one of my many friends.

Oh yeah. I was a cheater. The seven-year itch would strike me at about eighteen months. I could feel the urge to cheat coming on me, like a cold. I thought of myself as an overlapper, as opposed to a cheater. As soon as I felt the relationship ending, I'd start to put feelers out for a new one. It was kind of like moonlighting for another company because the place you currently work for is about to go under. So every eighteen months or so, I'd start looking for a new "job."

Overlapping is how I met my husband. I'm not proud, because I was in my twenties and I wasn't thinking of anyone but Sherri. (In fact, it took a baby to jar me out of that kind of thinking.) Even the woman who "overlapped" with my husband when I was pregnant—well, she was twenty-three. I remember being twenty-three, and I was self-centered and unthinking. It takes getting hurt before you have enough compassion not to hurt someone else.

Charlie. He was nice. He went to church. He had great parents. And sure enough, at eighteen months, I felt an itch. I was bored with Charlie. And when my hairdresser introduced me to his friend, who was back in town after being "away" (prison), well, dating him seemed like a good idea.

Exciting. Sexy. Prison.

Within a few dates, we were a couple. Me and Prison Guy. (Look, I don't learn from my mistakes until I make at least ten of them in a row.) I'm sorry to say I was too immature to properly break up with Charlie. I did to him what I did to everyone—I stopped calling. I disappeared for a week or two. It was, to quote Charlie's top complaint about me, "irresponsible." I was proving him right.

One day, I was hanging out with Prison Guy at my hairdresser's house. Having a good time.

I heard a knock. Prison Guy got the door.

"Sherri, there's a guy named Charlie here, says he's looking for his girlfriend," said Prison Guy.

I could not have been more surprised. Charlie had dropped me off at my hairdresser's a few times but I'd never dreamed he'd come there *looking* for me. And this situation, Prison Guy and Charlie, each looking at me like I'm his woman, could quickly deteriorate into a bad scene. Prison Guy was armed. He walked over to me while Charlie stood in the doorway.

"I will shoot this motherfucker," Prison Guy said. "Who is this guy, and why is he saying you're his girlfriend?"

I don't believe in telling a recently released felon that he's wrong, so I didn't tell him, "Technically, I am."

I decided to defuse the situation. I told Prison Guy to chill, that I would take care of it. I was barefoot, wearing a cute little outfit. I went to the door.

As soon as Charlie saw me, he yanked me out of the house and down the stairs. I didn't make a sound. If Prison Guy thought I was being kidnapped, he'd shoot Charlie. And I don't like my relationships to end in murder.

Charlie threw me into his Mazda RX-7 and peeled down the street. I was shocked. The nice guy! The teacher! Speeding down the 10 freeway, sobbing like a baby. "You broke my heart," he cried.

I was watching L.A. pass by me at seventy, eighty miles per hour, wondering if I could jump out of the car. Michael Douglas made it look so easy in *Romancing the Stone*, but then again, I thought I could haul Gilbert up a building with a bedsheet. I decided that if I jumped out of an RX-7 speeding down the I-10, not even dental records would be able to identify me.

I talked some sense into Charlie. I asked him to take me back to my hairdresser's so I could get my stuff (I was still barefoot). I told him that we'd be together, that I was so sorry—anything I could think of that would make this crazy man stop sobbing.

I kind of meant it, because in a weird way his behavior made me feel flattered. *Someone loves me so much he's actually lost his mind! Maybe if I survive this day,* I thought, *I should give "boring" Charlie another look.* But when we returned to the hairdresser's house, Charlie changed his mind. The second I stepped out of the car, he grabbed me and threw me back in. He knew I was lying. I probably took it one step too far with "We'll be together forever." He might've been dull, but he wasn't dumb.

Now we were tearing up the Pacific Coast Highway, replaying the same scene we had apparently been rehearsing on the I-10. He was driving and sobbing, I was praying and sobbing. Finally, he ran out of gas in Malibu. He pulled up to a gas station. A police car was parked across the road. I saw it, then Charlie saw me see it.

Before I could finish plotting my escape, he leaned down and said, "If you jump out of this car, I'm going to pour this gas all over you and set you on fire."

Instead of being worried for my life, I was worried for my outfit. This dress was new, I just got it out of layaway. And, again, the part of me that wasn't scared to death was flattered. *This man loves me so much, he done lost his mind.*

I sat quietly while Charlie filled up the car, preparing for a long drive.

We drove up a dark, twisty mountain road in the Pacific Palisades. All I could see was mountain on one side and ocean on the other. Both were lit by the sparks Charlie was creating by scraping the RX-7 against the guardrail. I was both terrified and excited. Yes, I can't swim and I've got my new outfit on, but he done love me so much, he done *lost his mind!*

I made a man *lose his mind!*

We ended up on a desolate mountain pass. I was sure we'd stumble on Mafia remains. I kept expecting to see a skeleton wearing a pinkie ring and a track suit. Charlie parked and got out of the car, still crying. I immediately locked all the doors. Charlie started banging on the window.

"Get out of the car, get out, Sherri, get out!"

"No! No way!" I shouted.

"Get. Out. Of. The. Car," he yelled. I could hear the wind whipping through the trees, wailing, *Whore, whore, whore.*

Then his voice changed, got softer. He coaxed, he pleaded. He got frantic. He said he was sorry. He grew hysterical. Anything

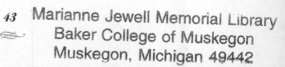

to get me out of the car. I thought to myself, *Girl, if you get out of this car, he's going to throw you off this mountain and no one will ever find you. They'll find your nice new outfit in tatters. Your carcass will be eaten by coyotes.*

Eventually I unlocked the car. We both calmed down. Charlie drove me to the hairdresser's house. I got my stuff. And if you've been paying attention, it will come as no surprise that Charlie and I stayed together for another six months. I told you I'm loyal, in my own way. When we did break up, I did it right. I sat him down, said those words I'd read in a thousand and one scripts. *"We have to talk. Things aren't working out. It's me, not you."* Turns out speaking the truth is a whole lot easier than sleeping with a felon.

Charlie and I broke up so well that we stay in touch—although the etiquette that goes along with being friends with an ex is still confusing to me. For example, I recently learned that if you're at a party with an ex and his wife, don't introduce him as your former boyfriend. Just say, "This is my friend Charlie and his wife." I understand why Charlie's wife wouldn't care for me telling strangers that I planted a flag on her man before she did. But it did make me a little sad. Now I can't tell people that this mild-mannered Clark Kent slipped into a phone booth, put on a Crazyman outfit, and took me on the scariest drive of my life because he was so in love with me that he done *lost his mind.*

Charlie and his wife have called to pray with me. I can understand why.

I did not remain friends with Prison Guy. He's back in jail, and at this stage in my life, I'm looking for Never Been to Prison Guy.

> *So write yourself a permission slip to let go of any man who loves you so much that he done lost his mind. Because that man has in fact done lost his mind, and you need to move on.*

Let's try a religious guy!

After Charlie, I dated an ultra-religious guy. Sheron prayed a *lot*. When we got in the car, Sheron said a prayer. When we pulled up to a stop sign, Sheron said a prayer. When we got out of the car, Sheron said a prayer. I'd tease him, "Sheron, don't you think God heard us back on the Ventura freeway?"

On the off chance that we hadn't pestered God enough, we also attended church three or four times a week. Religion was part of everything, including our sex life, which was celibate. And not that "Girl, we only have sex twice a month" celibate. No— Sheron and I were the real deal, as in "Girl, we never had sex once, not for the entire three years we were together" celibate. You read that right. Three years of celibacy. I probably lasted longer than some priests.

Being celibate is like being on a diet, and sex is like pizza. If you go without it for a few days, you realize you can go without it for a while. My time with Sheron taught me that real love means a man cares for your heart as much as he cares for your body. And it's possible that someone will think you are special without trying to sleep with you. Sheron and I had great talks. And some make-outs on the couch that would put a seventh-grader to shame. I learned how much more goes into a relationship than just sex.

But when Sheron started talking marriage, I just couldn't do it. Like Charlie, he was a Good Guy (both G's capitalized), but his extreme religious fervor made him judgmental in a way I found inhibiting.

When I was performing, the other comics could tell by the way I was watering down my act if Sheron was in the room. He disapproved of some of the more outrageous things I said, and he thought I laughed too loud. My dad didn't like Sheron, either.

"Sherri, he's breaking your spirit," Dad said.

I tend to attract serious guys who think I'll give them a little fun. But after a while, they want to return to their serious roots and take me with them. My dad would always tell me, "Sherri, you need someone who loves you for who you are, not some man who wants to tone you down."

Toward the end of my three-year relationship with Sheron, I returned to my overlapping ways. After all, I'd been celibate for almost an entire presidential term. My friend Jeff and I enjoyed each other's company. Instead of feeling guilty, I was impressed that my eighteen-month itch didn't appear until thirty-six months in. But when Sheron found out, like Charlie, he lost his mind.

Sheron didn't try to kill me, but he did start cursing me out. And the words he used that day were a thousand times worse than the ones I said onstage. Hell hath no fury like a Christian man scorned.

I should've known Sheron was possessive. One night we went to a movie and I commented on how gorgeous George Clooney was. I believe this is standard, red-blooded woman conversation. In fact, I'll say that having the hots for Clooney is every American woman's patriotic duty. We have to support American sex symbols by fantasizing about them, and Clooney is one of ours. Well, Sheron thought I was going to contact George Clooney and sleep with him. I told him that was ridiculous; how on earth would I get ahold of George Clooney? What I didn't tell Sheron was that I would sleep with George Clooney anytime, anyplace. The real obstacle was not my love for Sheron, but my inability to call George Clooney and inform him of my sexual availability. Sheron and I are friends, but I'm glad we didn't get married. Because we would be divorced.

> *So write yourself a permission slip to date a man who likes your laugh and realizes your desire for George Clooney is healthy and patriotic.*

Marrying my "overlap"

Being with Jeff made me happy, and not just because he broke a celibacy streak. But I was so desperate for this relationship to work that I blocked out the messages he was sending me. As I said earlier: Men will tell you who they are; it's up to us women to listen to them. Jeff told me at the beginning that not only was he unable to be monogamous, he didn't even want to try. He wouldn't be attending church, and if he saw a woman he wanted to date, he would do his best to make that date happen. He even warned me at the beginning, "Sherri, it's going to be three years before I can say I love you."

At year two, day three hundred and sixty-four, I pestered him. "Hello? Waiting for my three words!"

I got them, and all of a sudden we were officially in love. We got married. And I told myself, *If I just show Jeff how much I love him, he won't cheat.*

I was right for a while. But here's the thing: Men mean what they say and they say what they mean. Jeff told me who he was; I shut my eyes and cupped my hands over my ears and shouted "Nyah, nyah, I can't hear you." I believed what I wanted to believe, until I was forced to see the truth. Marriage is work. It's a cliché, but it's true. Before I got married, when I'd hear people say that, I'd say, "Well, *your* marriage is work. Mine's gonna be easy."

Riiiight.

We both failed. Jeff made wrong choices, so did I. Although his choices were a *tad* more wrong than mine, I did have to look at myself in the mirror and ask, *What could I have done better?*

None of us goes into a marriage thinking it's going to end in divorce. No matter how hardened our hearts may be, each of us wants someone we can trust. And we want to give that person everything. (Ironically, if you divorce, you will be giving that person everything.) But that's the leap of faith we take. And if you don't fully turn over your heart, then you're just loaning it. And you're doomed. I'm not even sure it's a mistake to pick the wrong guy. Maybe it's part of the process.

I never thought Jeff would betray me. He was my husband and my best friend. My coach, my cheerleader. Jeff would walk me through auditions, prepping me so I booked the job. He'd help me nail a character and make sure I found my funny. And Jeff could always talk me off a ledge.

The first time I appeared on *The Ellen DeGeneres Show,* I was a mess. Backstage, I was sweating and shaking, convinced I wasn't good enough. If I'd appeared on the show like that, I would've bombed and never been invited back. Jeff held my face and put his forehead on mine.

"You can do this," he said. "You are good enough. You will be fine."

When it was my time to saunter out on that stage and dance with Ellen, I was ready. And I was funny. Jeff even brought my wigs to the set, which, to me, is an act of truly heroic proportions. This man loved me. When I return to that question, *What could I have done better?* the answer is not as ethereal as you'd think.

I should've put out more.

One thing I loved about my celibacy is the way it forced the relationship to grow in another direction first. So when Jeff and I started dating, I pushed us in that direction. I held back sexually, telling him, "If we get married, the lid is coming off the freak!"

"You promise?" he'd say.

"I promise," I'd say. And I meant it. I was dying to be Sherri Superfreak—with the right person. Yes, we had sex during the five years that we dated, and it was good. However, I didn't want to abandon celibacy completely. I'd suggest it but I wouldn't insist on it because I didn't want to lose Jeff. I compromised my values.

We broke up a lot.

Even though things were rocky, I wanted that ring on my finger. Marriage was important to me. It was time. I believed that once we were married, the sex stuff would work itself out.

Riiiight.

As a wife, I wasn't nearly as freaky as I thought I'd be. Jeff would make a move and I'd rattle off excuses. *I'm tired. I gotta go to work, I gotta do the laundry, I gotta go get my hair done, I gotta make you coffee.* Sherri Superfreak got overwhelmed by Sherri Superwife.

> **Write yourself a permission slip to be the ho in matrimony that you wished you'd been when you were single.**

The parent trap

Also, we wanted to have a baby. After two years of trying the old-fashioned way, we decided to go the in-vitro route. And while I made time for sex during our attempts at "natural" conception, once we started fertility treatments, the sex stopped. It almost seemed pointless. Why have sex when it isn't working? My son's conception was the result of white lab coats, not black lingerie. The first time we went to the clinic, I watched, fully dressed, as my husband took a cup into a private room so he could look at naked ladies and make his half of the baby.

Jeff apparently took a long time. A nurse tapped on the door, asking how things were going.

"I can't even get a good groove going if you're gonna keep knocking," he shouted.

He complained about his reading material, which didn't activate his imagination. "Why am I looking at a *National Geographic*? What the heck am I supposed to do with *National Geographic*?"

The staff finally came around (no pun intended) and gave him a porno to watch. I didn't know whether to be proud or embarrassed. That's my man—he won't settle for *National Geographic*. The porno was actually an instructional sex video from the 1960s. No wonder I didn't get pregnant from that cup.

One time Jeff "got a sample" at home. It was my job to take it to the doctor. I cared for this cup of sperm like it was liquid gold that would save humanity. I put it in a paper bag, packing it on the front seat, and drove up a long, winding Los Angeles road called Beverly Glen. I took a curve too fast, and my gold fell off the seat. I almost lost control of the car, shouting to no one, "If this sperm is contaminated with carpet fibers I'm going to throw myself off this mountaintop right now!"

My sperm and I made it to the clinic fiber free. The waiting room was packed with all kinds of women, each carrying her man's sperm. So many samples of liquid gold, I was certain the cups were going to get switched. All I needed was to carry a baby that looked a little bit like me and not remotely like Jeff. And there'd be some white lady walking around with Jeff's baby in her belly. (Little did I know, that was about to happen.)

Despite Jeff's experience at the clinic, he had it easier than me. When I asked the doctor what else I could do to get pregnant, he didn't give me a picture of George Clooney and a key to the "sample" room. No, he told me to lose weight.

I started an Oprah-style liquid diet, and went from a size 14 to a size 2 in six months. I was under medical supervision, and I was dedicated. I've never lost weight that fast before or since. Jeff and I even went to Cabo San Lucas for a romantic vacation and I refused to eat solids. I was convinced that one bite of anything would send me on a binge. So I just drank. And not protein shakes, either—just piña coladas. On an empty stomach. Jeff envisioned our vacation as seven days of relaxation and lovemaking. I saw it as a week of sleep. And since I was dead drunk the whole time, it was.

Being a size 2 didn't make me pregnant. I had scar tissue, and the eggs weren't implanting in my uterus. I started getting hormone shots and seeing the doctor every three days. People were shoving things up my cooch on a regular basis. Cold things, sharp things—not the kinds of things that make you want to light a candle and get amorous with your husband. I often had to race home and lie on my back with my legs in the air for two days.

Jeff would give me that dead-eyed horny look, and I'd say, "Uh-uh. No sex. Air bubbles."

"Well, can you do an alternative?" he asked, referring to that act the church elders thought I was up to with Gilbert.

"No!" I'd say. "You want me to give you 'the alternative' while I got to lie on the couch with my legs up in the air? Oh no! Just turn on Jerry Springer and let me be!"

Eureka!

Two days before Thanksgiving—after a year and a half of fertility treatments—the doctor told me I was pregnant. With twins. And let me tell you, that is a terrifying thing to hear. Everything you've been thinking about, dreaming about, and planning for just doubled. Cribs: times two. Blankets: times two. Changing stations: times two. Clothes: times two. Onesies: times two. Money: times two. Panic: times ten.

I was scared to move, I didn't want to jostle the eggs. Even though the doctors cleared us to have sex, I couldn't do it. We'd worked so hard for these babies, I didn't want to jeopardize them (or make them feel unwelcome!). It's grown-up time, I told Jeff. We're about to have two children. We can't be hanging from chandeliers or swings like Pam Anderson and Tommy Lee. We're going to be *parents*. (I know that they're parents, but I didn't want Jeff to be a Tommy-Lee-kind-of-dad, and I didn't have the body to be a Pam-Anderson-kind-of-mom.)

After the pregnancy was confirmed, I got tunnel vision. I became oblivious to everything. Out of the corner of my eye, I saw that Jeff was starting to change, but I didn't want to face it, not at that time. I was pregnant and I had to keep these babies in me. Jeff started coming home late, and drinking, which was unusual for him.

When I was about eleven weeks along, I was walking a friend's dog, along with my dogs. Normally, three dogs were no problem. But today, my friend's little dog got feisty. Somehow, the leash got wrapped around my leg, and I fell flat on my back. I started bleeding immediately.

At the hospital, the doctors said, "Both of the embryos are surrounded by blood. You probably miscarried both of them. All we can tell you is to lie down and put both your legs up in the air."

We lost our daughter. It hit Jeff harder than it hit me. After a miscarriage, people typically rally around the mother. Everyone ignores the father. Men are taught to keep their chins up. Be strong for your wife. We don't let men cry. I still feel bad about that. Jeff got very little support from our friends. We grew even more distant.

> *So write yourself a permission slip this time—to pay attention the next time your man goes silent. He's telling you something.*

A hard pregnancy gets harder

I had placenta previa, which meant that the remaining embryo was sitting on top of my cervix. As the pregnancy progressed, the bleeding got worse. Jeff would walk into a bathroom that was covered in blood and clean it up. Every time it happened, we never knew if it was a miscarriage or just a bad day. We both felt helpless. Around this time, I sensed that something wasn't quite right with my husband. On April 20, two days before my birthday, I decided to ask him point-blank.

"Jeff," I said, "are you having an affair?"

He didn't say anything. Neither did I. My question hung in the air, waiting to land on an answer. Finally, after about forty-five seconds, Jeff gave one.

"Yes."

I went into shock. Depression. I stopped eating, stopped drinking anything, even water. I hadn't yet bonded with the baby in my body because I didn't know if he'd "stick." I cursed at Jeff, "Why did you let me get pregnant?"

A day later, on the twenty-first, I started having labor pains. I delivered Jeffrey three and a half months early, on my birthday. He weighed one pound, ten ounces.

A brief fling with insanity

Shortly after Jeffrey's birth, I was at home, reading the Bible. Things looked bleak. My preemie baby was in the neonatal intensive care unit, and my husband and I were barely speaking. Everything felt wrong. I was hoping to find some answers. Instead I heard a voice.

"Check his computer."

Now, I often hear God talking to me, but this was definitely not God's voice. So I ignored it and plowed on through Genesis.

"He's asleep. Just take a peek. What's the harm?"

I have never been the type to snoop. If my husband told me he was doing a show that night and wouldn't be back until 3 AM, I'd say, "Have a great set." If he called me to say, "I'm gonna stay over at The Comedy Store tonight, honey," I'd say, "Snuggle up!"

So reading his e-mail wasn't like me. But that voice kept interrupting my Bible study. I thought, *Let me just silence that voice so I can read the Lord's word.*

I checked my husband's inbox. I was looking for her. And I found her. He had pictures of the two of them together. I knew she existed, but I hadn't known what she looked like. Now I did. She looked like J.Lo, if J.Lo was white.

Not helpful.

For the first time since Jeff had confessed, I felt rage. A haze of red, followed by a near blackout. I returned to my desk and closed my Bible.

"God," I said. "I'll be right back."

I wasn't abandoning God, I just didn't want Him to see what I was about to do. God's got a lot going on, I figured, He doesn't need to see me murder my husband. What if He gets called to testify against me? It would be awkward.

I went into the living room. Jeff was sleeping on the couch. So peaceful, so unaware.

"I'm going to kill you," I said. He did not respond, which I took as a sign that Jeff was okay with that.

A lamp on the table caught my eye. I needed something to bash his head in, and that seemed like it would do the trick.

God tapped me on the shoulder.

"You cannot do this. You will go to jail."

"Lord, that's fine," I said, trying to reassure Him. "If that's my calling and my destiny, I accept it. I will go to jail and preach to the other inmates. 'Cause he's going to die. Right now."

I lifted the lamp, but it was too light. Now I understand why people buy antiques. They're heavy. The base of an old lamp can crush a skull. The base of a lamp from a trendy retailer can't even crush a fly. I looked at my husband's chest, rising and falling so easily. He had no idea.

"Call Earlene," God said.

I began to worry that His next sign would be a thunderbolt, so I grabbed my phone, ran to the driveway, and dialed.

"Earlene," I said, "I'm about to kill my husband. God told me to call you. But make no mistake. I am going back in that house and I'm going to find something to bash his head in."

I started making a mental inventory of all the furniture in our house that would crush Jeff's skull. *The television, the table—*

"Lord," said Earlene, "give her strength. Don't let her do this. Heal the marriage!"

I said nothing. *The ottoman, the printer, if I slammed it down real hard—*

"In Jesus Christ's name, amen," she finished.

"Amen," I heard myself say.

I didn't kill Jeff after all. I did empty out our bank account. And cancel all his credit cards. The bank almost didn't let me take the money because both of our names were on the account.

"I can't help you, ma'am," said the teller. "You have a different last name and you don't have any ID on you."

"Look," I said, "I just found out my husband has been cheating on me with another woman. And last night, I saw pictures."

She paused for a second, then asked, "How much do you need?"

> ***Write yourself a permission slip to
> celebrate the things you haven't done—
> like murder. Good for you!***

"*Working through it*"

Jeff and I decided to work on the marriage. Our son had just come home from the NICU. I couldn't believe I was going to be one of those women who stayed after adultery. I remembered how ada-mant I'd been a few years earlier.

"There's some things I'm not going to put up with," I'd warned Jeff, my neck rocking and rolling. "I'm not going to accept nobody cheating on me. Nuh-uh. You cheat on me, I'm out the door."

But when you have a child together, and common aspirations and dreams, well, that door is pretty heavy.

You have got to be kidding me

It was about this time that we found out the "other woman" was pregnant. Imagine the scenario. I've just been told that my son, whom I spent eighteen months trying to conceive and almost mis-carried every day, might be severely disabled. And along comes my husband's one-month stand, a white woman who gets preg-nant effortlessly. And who will probably have an easy pregnancy and a "normal" child.

I checked at Borders, Barnes & Noble. There are plenty of books about forgiving your partner, moving on. The books always say: Get away from the "other woman." Unfortunately, no one wrote a book called *She Got Pregnant at the Same Time I Was Pregnant and Now Our Sons Are Brothers.*

Someone should write that book, because I would buy it.

We decided to divorce right before I moved to New York. I ran out of steam. Jeff is the type of guy who tends to shut down when there's a lot of drama; yet I'd remind him about his mistake all the time.

"Now you got two baby-mamas," I'd say, getting my neck going. "You better get used to drama, Jeff. You created it."

Every day, I'd come up with new ways to remind Jeff that he'd cheated on me and didn't use condoms. I'd wake up in the morning and instead of asking, "What do you want for breakfast?" I'd say, "You didn't think about that when you had her lying up there naked, did you?!"

It's hard for a guy to answer, "Pancakes."

We saw a counselor, but he spent the entire hour putting out fires from the previous week. Sharing your man with another woman requires too much generosity. I don't know how sister-wives in polygamist marriages keep from yelling all day. Maybe all the free babysitting takes the edge off. But I wasn't able to swing it. Jeff was at White J.Lo's beck and call. He was at her side when she gave birth. If *their* son had to go to the doctor, Jeff would leave *our* son so he could take him. I was either yelling at Jeff, or yelling at White J.Lo.

I was so good at being angry, I could multitask through my rage. Once, White J.Lo called when I was getting a manicure and asked me not to attend her and my husband's son's birthday party, because she was a private person and didn't want her family knowing her business. She said that she only wanted my husband and Jeffrey to attend. As you can imagine, that did not go over well. At the nail salon, I alternated between yelling at White J.Lo and slow-talking to the Korean girl cutting my cuticles.

"Well," I said, "you should've thought of that before you got with my husband!"

The manicurist looked up, startled.

"Sorry! Her, not you," I said, pointing to the phone. "You're great!" I gave her a thumbs-up. Or thumb-up. She had my other thumb in her hand.

"I don't work at Ralph's! I'm on TV!"

"Oh, sweetie, don't cut the nails, just paint and file, please. Thank you.

"You should have thought about that when you were taking off your clothes for a married man.

"Red. I want a deep, deep red.

"Listen, when you sleep with somebody else's man, what do you think you're gonna get?

"Yeah, that looks good. What shade is that? I'll take a bottle.

"Oh, you think it's rude for me to talk to someone else when you're talking to me, too? Why, do you feel CHEATED ON? Give me a break!"

I was getting really good at being angry. Every day, I wanted Jeff to be grateful that I took his cheating ass back. I was turning into one of those women who's always popping out of bushes, trying to catch her man with another woman.

"What you doing?!"

"Fixing the car."

"With who?"

"No one!"

"Then whose perfume do I smell?"

"Yours!"

> *Write yourself a permission slip that says, "I tried, and I can't handle this."*

Moving on

We were arguing all the time in front of our son, Jeffrey. (I never call him Jeff.) One day I just looked at my husband and said, "I'm tired."

That's when I asked for a divorce. Jeff fought it. He wanted to keep the family together—this family was his idea, really. Jeff wanted kids; I was ambivalent. I'd seen so many of my girlfriends get pregnant and watch their men trip out, tune out, or just leave. I knew too many single mothers who were chasing down child support and trying to get the baby-daddy to visit the kid. I always swore, "No way that's gonna be me."

My divorce taught me that I don't need a man to validate me. I can do this, life, on my own. When Jeff and I broke up, one of my closest friends came to see me at the hotel where I was staying and asked me point-blank: "What are you afraid of?"

I started rattling off the list in my head. "Being alone. Raising my son by myself. Being a single mom. Making mistakes with Jeffrey. Nobody will want me."

"Hold up, girl," she said. "One day at a time. Figure out what you need to do *today*. Stop bringing up tomorrow. Don't borrow trouble."

She was right. And all the things I was afraid I couldn't do without a man? Now I'm doing them. (Except riding a motorcycle. But I may try that after my son graduates from college.) At home, Jeff took care of "guy" things like putting up shelves and moving furniture. There was always air in the tires and gas in the car. Once he was gone, I realized that I could do those things, too. I can book my own jobs, and give myself a pep talk. I even put my son's IKEA high chair together by myself. (It sounds like such a little thing, but for me it was a huge deal. The directions were in Swedish.) I hooked up my computer and I got the cable working by myself.

It wasn't a simple transformation, and it occurred slowly. When I moved to New York, I took seven girlfriends with me for the transition. The day they left, I cried like a baby. How was I going to take the subway by myself? I'm a California girl, I don't take trains, I drive. Good Lord, what if I ended up in the Bronx?

And the first time I took the subway by myself, I did get lost. But instead of being murdered, I simply got out at the next stop, hailed a cab home, and lived to write about it.

You don't know you can do something difficult until you do it, because it's *in* the doing that you find your strength. I love being on my own. No matter how bad things get, after I finish crying, I realize God is still there. And I feel Him saying, "I'm still with you, I'm still going to take care of you. Put one foot in front of the other."

Now I tell my girlfriends what Eddie Griffin once told me: "Even though you don't think you can . . . you can. And you will. Even if you have to do it scared."

> *Write yourself a permission slip to make a choice: Let the anger go, or the man. You can't live with both.*

The only man in my life

Living in New York has literally terrified me at times. The first time I took Jeffrey on the subway, I thought, *There is no way this is going to work.* He was in a stroller and we had to descend three flights of stairs. But I had no choice. The platform was crowded for rush hour, so I bellowed, "Excuse me, excuse me, stroller coming through!" Down the stairs we came, like a pair of real New Yorkers. Until I got lost, again.

"Jeffrey," I said, "Mommy took the wrong train. Or the right train the wrong way. Dang."

We made a game out of it and found our way home. I promised my son, "We are going to have a great time in this city."

Being alone has taught me so much. But I've learned from each man I've been with, too—even the bad ones. Especially the bad ones. Despite how awfully some of my relationships ended, I'm friends with many of my exes. Even Jeff and I are on good terms. And he overlapped on me! Jeff and I were friends long before we were a couple. We make each other laugh. People see us together and don't believe we're divorced.

Being single this time has taught me that sisters need to enjoy their season of singleness. Marriage is not the cure to loneliness; in fact, it's often the cause. Whatever you are, you will attract. I spent a lot of my single years being angry, and I dated some angry guys. Once I had dinner with a guy whose credit card was declined. I offered to use my card, and surprise, surprise, it was declined, too.

So how do you get around all this? My real-world suggestion for every single woman out there is: Get yourself some property. You can get some great deals now, and nothing focuses your mind like a mortgage. When you have a home and thirty-year commitment to a bank, suddenly you get real selective. Some guy lives with his mother? "Sorry, your mama and my mortgage payment don't mix." And when a guy says he's serious, make him prove it. "You want me? Rake my leaves. Clean my pool filter. And pull that dead squirrel out from under my porch.

"Then I'll believe you're serious."

I can sum up what men have taught me in ten words: God protects stupid people, do it scared, buy a house.

Men are mistakes waiting to be made. You have to admit, every guy seems like a good idea at the time. I think this chapter should end with "to be continued," because I'm not done yet. My gut tells me I have a few more lessons to learn from those creatures. So, I'll probably be dating a few more wrong guys, just to stay sharp. If I can do it, so can you.

> ***Write yourself a permission slip to love the wrong guy. Just don't marry him.***

part three

Permission to Pursue Your Dreams

Can you fall in love with an experience? Because that's what happened to me the first time I performed stand-up comedy. It was like stand-up took me out for a date, spent the night at my house, and gave me ten back-to-back orgasms. He left before I woke up. All I got was a note saying, "You were great, you should try me again."

I was one of those kids who was always putting on a show. My specialty was the post–Kingdom Hall Sunday revue. My whole family would get together after church, and us kids would put on a talent show. My cousins, my sisters, and I would sing, dance, recite poetry. My grandmother Mary used to nudge me, "Go do your little program."

I'd sing, but I wasn't a good singer, which is probably how I got my first laughs. Stand-up comedy wasn't on my radar when I was a kid, but the radio was. I'd put the fan next to my radio and sing, because the fan made my voice quiver.

Making the haters laugh

My ambitions were vague—I wanted to do something big. I never thought being funny would be my "big" thing, but as a kid, I used humor to defuse racial tension. The Chicago suburb where I grew up was white, and, in case your copy of this book does not have a cover, I am not. In school, I generally got picked last for things. One time, a girl got stuck with me on her track team.

"I don't want no nigger on my team," she complained.

I don't remember what I said, but somehow I made her laugh. Unfortunately, that wasn't an isolated incident. I heard it enough that making the N-word offender laugh became my official policy. Not that it cured anybody of saying it. Often my hard work would be rewarded with, "Oh, that nigger is so funny."

That's probably why I get upset when white people use that word, no matter what the context. I can take the N-word from black people because I know where they're coming from. But when a white person uses it, I'm gonna get upset. And now you understand why. I've expressed my thoughts about it many times on *The View.*

> *Write yourself a permission slip to hold firm on a gut feeling, even if someone else can explain it away.*

A dream is born

I'd never considered trying stand-up comedy until I saw it live. My girls—other legal secretaries—and I decided to treat ourselves to a night on the town. The eight of us took up a table at The Comedy Store, a club on Sunset Boulevard in Hollywood. Before the show had started, I was being myself, yakking it up, making my friends laugh, making people at other tables laugh.

The show started, and Andrew Dice Clay took the stage. Now, I have no problem telling you that Andrew is a very nice man who's really funny. However, on that night, he was extremely offensive. He was Hickory Dickory Docking, Clickity Clockity Cocking, pissing off entire tables of women. Several ladies who were entertained by my pre-show at the table turned around and said, "You're funnier than he is. You should do that."

And the first seed was planted—while Dice was rhyming *witch* in some poor woman's face.

Eddie Griffin was the headliner. That's when I saw comedy bring an audience together. Literally, people rocked back and forth as a single unit. Eddie was talking about things everyone could relate to, but I could hardly pay attention because I kept watching the audience react to him.

Seeing one man making so many people laugh. The second seed—planted.

I approached Eddie after the show.

"I want to try this. Can you give me any advice?" I asked.

I didn't realize that was an opening line for groupies, too, so Eddie started hitting on me.

"Do you want to sleep with me?" he asked.

"No! I really want advice," I said.

He could've brushed me off—there were other girls who did

want to sleep with him, standing behind me—but instead, he encouraged me to give it a shot.

"But what if I'm scared," I asked him.

"If you're scared, do it scared."

I doubt if Eddie realized that he'd just given me a philosophy for the rest of my life. To this day, I do things scared. Every morning when the announcer says, "Please welcome the ladies of *The View*," I'm doing it scared, hoping I don't accidentally say the moon is made of cheese. I should have my own athletic shoe with Nike. Instead of Olympians, my commercial would show me, on *The View*, talking politics with Barbara Walters. Do it scared.

When I got home from The Comedy Store that night, I called up a girlfriend.

"Do you think I could do that?" I asked.

"Sherri, don't do it. It's going to take you ten years. You're going to be struggling, you're not going to make any money," she said, being realistic.

I called another.

"No, Sherri. You got your pension plan, your 401(k) is good, you're making thirty grand with overtime, you are set," she said, being practical.

One by one, I dialed through the secretary pool, and I kept getting the same advice. Finally, I reached my friend Dianetta.

"No one wants me to try comedy," I said.

"Sherri, if you don't try, you'll never know," Dianetta said.

That must've been the answer I was waiting for, because that was my last call. The third seed had been planted. Now I had a garden to grow.

Dianetta loaned me six hundred dollars to take a comedy class with Judy Carter. (She still teaches, if you're interested.) Judy didn't like any of my material, but she liked my personality. My first time onstage was, as I said, orgasms and epiphanies. The club was the L.A. Cabaret, and I packed the house with allies. Everyone from my law firm came—the secretaries, the lawyers, and probably a few defendants.

I can't remember a word I said, but the audience was rocking back and forth, just like they had when Eddie was onstage. I was killing. I killed.

> *Oh, this one's easy. Write yourself a slip to do it scared.*

A distraction from difficult circumstances

Comedy quickly became the only part of my life I truly enjoyed. My mom was in and out of the hospital with diabetes, and my boyfriend was in prison. Telling jokes was the only thing that calmed me down. Comedy became for me, as it does for every comedian, the thing I lived for. I'd go to two or three clubs a night, and because my car had been repossessed, I'd take the bus to my shows.

Open mics are the wretched beginnings of every comedian's career. I'd sign up at a pizza parlor. As the hours ticked by, the emcee would start seeing me eye my watch. I had a bus to catch. He'd say, "Okay, Sherri, you're next." Then he'd get up onstage.

"Ladies and gentlemen, are you ready for your next comedian?"

I'm thinking the next words out of his mouth are going to be "Sherri Shepherd."

"Arlo Thomas!" he'd say.

And Arlo would walk onstage, meaning I would be stuck at the pizza place for another fifteen minutes, at least. *There goes that bus.*

"I thought I was next," I'd say.

"You are, you're next."

"Next" has its own meaning at an open mic, and it's almost never "next." But you can't leave the venue, because at some point you are next. And since you just spent three hours poring over your notes at the back of a pizza parlor, what's another ten minutes? Often, famous comedians stop by open mics to try new material. Sometimes they perform for hours. I'm not naming names, but every time Marlon Wayans walked onstage, I could've gone to dinner and a movie and returned in time to hear Marlon telling the audience "Good night."

Much to my dismay, Armageddon is a ways off

In those days, my car was in a constant state of repo. The Witnesses had drilled into my head the notion that Armageddon was coming. The end of the world, *possibly tomorrow*! Throughout my twenties, my financial motto was, "Why am I paying bills? Armageddon is coming." The Witnesses probably just wanted me to keep coming to church, but I used Jesus's Second Coming as an excuse to blow off parking tickets.

One night, I was on my way to my show at The Comedy Store. Although I was currently in possession of my car, that was about to change. I had a glove compartment full of tickets, the car was not registered, and I was driving with no insurance. I used to purchase what I called "Survivor's Insurance." Basically, you buy a policy. The company sends you a proof-of-insurance card, and then you cancel the check. When a cop pulls you over, at least you have the insurance card. It's probably impossible to do now because of electronic banking, but in the nineties, a girl could get away with that stuff.

A police car pulled up to the left of me. This happened frequently because the car had been wrecked. The driver's-side door was bashed in, and the window was missing. To exit the vehicle, I had to climb out like Daisy Duke. And when it rained, I wore a garbage bag on my left arm. It was impossible for a cop not to pull up alongside me and at least take a good look.

I played it cool. It didn't work.

The police car dropped back and began tailgating me. Crap. I knew where this was headed so I drove into a mini-mall and threw my key under the mat. At least at a mall, my car wouldn't get towed. Because Lord only knew how long it would be before I could get it.

The cop pulled up behind me and ran my plates. The minutes dragged by. *This is taking too long,* I thought. Finally, he walked that slow cop-walk and leaned into my window.

"Ma'am, you'll need to step out of the car."

I edged myself out through the window area as gracefully as possible. I was dressed in my "comedy" outfit, which was, unfortunately, influenced by Julia Roberts's character Vivian in *Pretty Woman*. My boots were thigh-high, my skirt was mini, and my cleavage was plunging. Vivian, you'll recall, was a prostitute.

"Ma'am, you're under arrest."

I died a little inside. All the shopowners came out of their stores at the mini-mall. They were all Asian, which, as a black woman, made things twice as embarrassing. I died some more inside. The cop drove me to the Van Nuys police station.

My one phone call was to a girlfriend. "Get my car and call my mom 'cause they're about to put me in jail," I sobbed.

In the pokey

This was Friday night. They stuck me with a bunch of other women, all of whom had been arrested for prostitution. Because of my outfit, I blended right in. We were handcuffed to a bench. There was plenty of complaining from the ladies.

"Shut up," snapped a cop. "Don't say nothing, just shut up."

Instead of talking, I tried to communicate my horror with my eyes. I was hoping that someone, anyone, would realize that I was not a prostitute and uncuff me from this bench of ill repute.

"I'm not like these other girls that I'm chained up next to," I thought to one cop.

Nothing.

"I'm a legal secretary in Beverly Hills. This is all a big mistake!" I thought to another.

Nothing.

Apparently my outfit, my stage makeup, and my crooked wig made my eye-pleas look like silent propositions.

They booked me. I was supposed to be taken to Rampart, a county jail that would later be embroiled in scandal involving, among other things, detainee abuse. But Rampart was full, so I stayed at Van Nuys.

I was terrified. I'd seen a thousand cop shows, that series *Cell Block H*. I was certain I'd have to fight someone, and I'm not a fighter. All my life, I'd used my humor on white girls, not my fists on prostitutes. I was going to be murdered, or at least beaten to pieces.

Lord, I prayed, *if You are thinking about launching Armageddon, now would be a great time.*

I was put in a cell with thirteen other women. It was the Friday before Martin Luther King Jr. Day, which meant I wouldn't see a judge until Tuesday. That was the only time I ever regretted that

MLK Jr. was given a national holiday. The staff didn't let us wash for the entire three-day weekend. When I finally got to shower, that water fell on my head like manna from Heaven.

I was shocked that the women in my cell were nice. No one jumped me; I did not get shanked. Tuesday morning came, and it was time to go to the courthouse. I had four or five "failure to appears," which is four or five too many. I was chained and cuffed to another woman. The two of us looked like a Siamese-twinned Hannibal Lecter. We were loaded, with other "couples," into a black-and-white prisoner bus. During the ride over, I was trying to catch the eye of pedestrians, drivers: "I'm a legal secretary. This is a mistake." But no one would look at me. It was such a lonely feeling. Even now, if I see a prison bus, I will look those people in the eye, wave, and say, "Hey!"

For that week, I spent all day at a court, and all night in jail. I called my boss as soon as I could on Tuesday.

"Hi Sandy, it's me Sherri. I'm in jail. Do I have any vacation days left?" I said.

"You got a week," she said.

"I'm taking it," I said.

I was sent to the Sybil Brand Institute for Women, which has since been torn down. I called my mom to let her know I'd been transferred and my sister Lori yelled into the phone, "Don't pick up the soap! Whatever you do, don't pick up the soap!" Lori, too, had watched a lot of *Cell Block H*.

The daily searches at Sybil Brand were humiliating and invasive. The worst was being forced to do the "squat and cough"—some women stored crack pipes in their "back pocket." Others hid crack pipes under their breasts, which is why I had to lift mine up.

Despite feeling dehumanized, I fell back on my instincts and made the people around me laugh. One guard got angry.

"You think this is funny?" she said.

"No," I said, not convincing her.

"Tell me this," she said. "Tell me how funny it is when you don't eat!"

I was not fed that day. And after about six hours, I stopped being funny.

The jail takes your clothes and replaces them with a grayish muumuu and a pair of panties. Each prisoner gets a bag with a tiny bar of soap, a mini-deodorant, and a comb. And that's it.

I felt disgusting.

Prison pals

About five days into my stay at this giant women's facility, I was aching to see a man. I noticed a janitor mopping the floor outside my cell. He wore a uniform and his hair was braided, like Buckwheat's. He wasn't handsome, but he was male, and I needed to feel feminine again. He smiled at me.

"How you doing," he asked.

I started crying. He came in my cell and sat on my bed.

"This is a mistake," I sobbed, finally able to tell my story with something other than my eyes. "I'm not supposed to be here."

"Are you hungry?" he asked.

"I'm starving!" I said.

"I'm gonna go get you a Snickers," he said.

He left. Apparently there were vending machines nearby.

"Excuse me," said a voice behind me. I turned around, and there was a large black woman stretched out on a bottom bunk, her hands clasped behind her head.

"Yes?"

"You do know that's a woman, right?" she said.

"He's a woman?" I said.

"*She* is a woman. And if you eat that Snickers bar," she said, "the next thing you're gonna be eating is that coochie."

"Oh my God," I said, sick to my stomach. I curled up in a ball. "What am I gonna do?"

"I don't know. But if you eat that Snickers bar"—she shrugged—"you gonna be her wife."

The man (okay, woman—well, how about wo-man?) came back. She sat on my bed. Never in my life did a Snickers bar look so menacing.

"No thank you. I'm not like that," I cried. "I only said yes because I was hungry!"

"F-you," she said, angry. "You're way too much trouble."

She left and "gave the Snickers bar" to someone else. Later I found out that a different girl rebuffed her advances, and when that girl fell asleep, the wo-man punched her in the mouth.

Yvette was the lady who'd warned me about the wo-man, and we are still friends. Yvette looked out for me during the rest of my stay at Sybil Brand. She was feared—she'd beat up a vagrant who stole her drugs.

"Leave Sherri alone," Yvette told people, "because she's gonna be somebody. We going to be here for the rest of our f'ing lives."

Yvette was wrong about herself. Yvette did get out of jail; she's now head of security at a building in Burbank. Yvette wore a skullcap to my wedding, and her girlfriend was as white and pink as a Barbie doll. Someone asked me, "Who is that woman you invited to your wedding?"

"That's my Yvette," I said.

Saved by Yvette

Since we were only allowed one pair of underpants, I'd wash mine at night and drape them over my bed to dry. One morning, I woke up and my panties were missing. As soon as I noticed, the cell instigator, known as Lil Bit, started instigating.

"Girl," Lil Bit said to me, "I know who stole your panties!"

"Okay," I said.

"Bertha stole your panties! Bertha stole your panties!" she said.

Other women started to gather around. They wanted a fight, I could feel it.

"Bertha got your panties," Lil Bit shrieked. "What you gonna do?"

Shoot. Bertha was already angry with me. Earlier in the week, she had been touching my hair. My real hair. (Of course I had to surrender my wig.)

"You got beautiful hair," Bertha had said. "You got beautiful hair."

It didn't *seem* sexual. Of course, this is coming from someone who couldn't tell a man from a woman. I assumed that when Bertha commented on my "beautiful hair," it meant she wasn't going to kill me. So I'd let her keep petting my head.

Yvette had cornered me after Bertha left.

"Stop letting her play with your hair."

"Why?" I asked.

"Sit down," Yvette had said, shaking her head, not even explaining. She gave me emergency cornrows, which kept Bertha at bay. Bertha had taken them as a diss.

Now I was looking at Bertha's bed. Two pairs of panties were lying across it.

"Bertha." I walked up to her, stammering. "Uh, my panties seem to be missing and I was wondering if you saw them."

"I ain't seen your motherfuckin' panties," she said.

"Okay, thank you," I said, and I went right back to my bed. I didn't make Bertha laugh, but I didn't get beat up. At that moment, jail stopped being a crazy adventure. I just wanted out. And all I had to do was finish out the week without underpants.

Almost every day I was taken to a different court. (I spread my "failures to appear" around.) One day, I went to the Beverly Hills courthouse. Normally, prisoners are taken to court in a service elevator. But the Beverly Hills guards were jerks and they took me up in the normal elevator, which is the one that the attorneys use. Of course, I was trying to say with my eyes, "I'm one of y'all, I'm a secretary. I work down the block!" But I was chained, my hair bound in Yvette's tight cornrows, looking like a stone-cold murderer. My eye-pleas only convinced people I was saying, "You're next."

Beverly Hills turned out to be my final stop. After a long day of waiting, I stood up before my last judge.

"Young lady, what are you doing here?" he asked.

"I'm a legal secretary and I didn't know about my warrants and these ladies stole my panties," I blurted.

"Are you going to pay your warrants?" he asked.

"Yes, sir," I sniffled.

And that was that. My time was served and I was released that night. Now if I ever get a parking ticket, a bill, anything—I take care of it immediately. Jesus may indeed be coming back one day, but it appears that He's waiting until I pay off my credit cards.

> *So write yourself a permission slip to stay on top of your finances. Because vacation days go by real slow in jail.*

Released on my own recognizance

I returned to comedy a hardened criminal, but that didn't help me with the black audience. I grew up around white people, which is why I'm comfortable around them. White audiences are nice, they have an open mind, they listen. "Okay, what does she have to say?" They give a comedian time to settle in and be funny. I did much better at white clubs. You get a three-second grace period in front of a white audience, which doesn't sound like much but is actually four seconds longer than you get at a black club.

"You ain't cute! I don't know what you think you're doing!"

Black audiences at a black comedy club respond to a rhythm—boom, boom, boom, boom—more than they respond to individual jokes. Their attitude toward comedians is practical. Like, "You better be worth the money I just spent. I didn't pay a cover charge and then buy two watered-down Hennessys so you could have a three-second grace period. You better be funny *now*."

The black clubs were the hardest for me. They honed my wit. I had to put aside my jokes and improvise. Audience members would get high outside the club, walk in the room, and shout, "I'm going to make your show better."

They would even try to get onstage with me, which is dangerous. When you're onstage, you can't see anything but the lights, then all of a sudden a stoned idiot steps up and grabs your mic? It's scary. And the security guards never did a thing to stop it. Once I complained and the bouncer broke it down for me.

"Look, if he ain't hit you, he fine. He all right."

"But you're supposed to do something," I said.

"He buyin' drinks. He ain't hit you, right? He didn't hit you?"

"No."

"He all right," he said. "Do your thing. Do your thing."

If you have to get hit before management gets concerned, you either learn to defuse the situation, or you get hit.

I kept journals of all my sets, and I have pages and pages about bombing. I can still see the tearstains—I was struggling to find my voice. I'd see successful black female comedians take the stage like boxers. Their attitude was like, *I'm not playing with you. I will fight you. I will. Try it with me.*

They put the audience in their place right away, and they would kill.

Well, that's not me. I'm not a tough girl, I'm not from "the streets" unless you count cul-de-sacs. And as you know, I'd rather walk around jail with no underpants on than get in a fight.

When I tried to act tough, the black audiences would sniff me out instantly. I talked like a Valley Girl and as soon as I smiled, it was over. The bombing continued, and it was getting more and more painful to perform. Other comedians would avoid me like my "condition" was contagious, and if they talked to me they would bomb, too.

Chesticles

I started writing heckler lines ahead of time, to prepare for the black crowds. One problem I had was actually two. My breasts. They are large, and people feel like they can comment on them as soon as I take the stage. Like me being a comedian gives them some kind of diplomatic immunity and they can be rude.

If I didn't acknowledge my chest immediately, the audience would get restless. *Does she know how big her breasts are?* Invariably, someone would shout, "Damn! Look at those titties!"

I'd catch men in the act of staring at them all the time. At the law firm, I really couldn't say anything. But onstage, I could call them out.

"Don't look down there, the jokes ain't coming from my boobs, they coming out of my mouth, look up."

I'd disarm the women: "You got a little appetizer, but mine is like a whole buffet. You can put mine in a refrigerator and warm them up in the microwave and they'd still be good."

Still, the black audiences were much more vocal about my breasts, and they did not let go of the topic just because I'd told a few jokes. One night, I cooked up a great heckler line. All I had to do was deliver it with complete, tough-girl confidence and the audience would be mine.

My plan was, no matter what a guy said about my chest, to say, "You so broke, you couldn't even afford my breasts. You have to put my breasts on layaway." (Now, this was back in the 1990s, before Visa started giving credit to everyone. If you wanted something that was too expensive, you put it on layaway.)

So there I was, onstage at the Townhouse in Inglewood. And this is the night that the pimps brought their hoes to the show. This is a demanding audience. This is their equivalent of a lunch break; they go right back to work after the show. I had to bring it.

Someone heckled me. I summoned my inner ho and said, "You couldn't. You. Uh. My titties got . . . to be on layaway!"

I'd fumbled the ball at the Super Bowl. The audience stood up, the pimps and their hoes, and started doing that Apollo thing.

"BOO! BOO!" Their hands pointing to the part of the stage where they would like me to go—off. I couldn't talk over their boos. I still wince thinking of that walk of shame to the bathroom.

D. L. Hughley was the host. He found me afterward, crying. "Sherri," he said, "you have to get back up on that stage. Come back next week and get up on that stage."

I didn't want to hear it. The audience had won. I had been crushed, and I wanted to surrender forever.

But I took D.L.'s advice and I came back the next week. And I killed.

If black rooms were my comedy meat, gay rooms were the dessert. Gay men love black women. I'd perform at cabarets in West Hollywood. A club called The Rage used to have a Gong Show. I won it twenty or twenty-five times—I hold the record. The winner got a hundred dollars and I'd always win, unless a big black gospel singer showed up. Then I was doomed. The law of the universe is that a regular-size black woman will never beat a fat black woman, especially if that fat lady sings.

I should point out that a "white" club is actually just a mainstream comedy club. Once I was booked at a redneck bar. The backdrop to the stage was a Confederate flag. There were three black people at the show, me and two of my secretary friends, whom I'd brought along for protection. My material at that time revolved around my boobs, and the trials and tribulations of dating an African. Not exactly tapping into a common experience.

Yet they laughed. I had a great set. At the end of the show, all these skinhead guys showed us their motorcycles. Having my girlfriends at the show made all the difference. I have tried to share my success with the secretaries—they are partially responsible for it. One friend from the law firm survived breast cancer. Well, she got booked on *The View* to talk about her experience.

> ***Write yourself a permission slip to bring your friends on your journey, especially if your journey detours into a biker bar.***

Day job blurs into night job

As much as I loved the women at the firm, the actual job of showing up to work every day was killing me. Not only did I try to hit two or three clubs per night, but I was taking the bus to each one. And the bus in L.A. is not like the bus in New York. It's the last resort. If you are on an L.A. bus, something in your life didn't go right. Because Los Angeles wants you and your dream, but you are expected to show up with a car. And if you don't have one, you're either illegal or poor. (Or in possession of a hundred unpaid tickets.) So, to placate people like me, the city threw together this bus system at the last minute, and it sucks.

A thirty-minute trip would take hours. I wouldn't get home from my shows until two or three in the morning. Not on weekends, but weeknights. And I lived in downtown L.A., on 6th and Alvarado. Walking through parks late at night, passing by crackheads, drug dealers, and the homeless, dressed like a prostitute. I'd be so tired in the morning, I'd grab whatever clothes were on the floor. Occasionally, I'd grab my comedy outfit. One day my boss, Sandy, took me aside.

"I can't have you dressing like that," she said, pointing to my chest. I looked down, and all I saw were the tops of my breasts, busting out of my halter top.

"Sorry," I said.

When I started comedy, I dressed like a nerd. Tootsie glasses, overalls, bobby socks, and tennis shoes. I started seeing female comedians who didn't dress "funny," they dressed *up*. And that's when I bought the thigh-highs, the miniskirts, and some wigs. A lot of wigs.

Wig women

That hair you see on *The View* is my own in the same way that the breasts you see on *The Hills* are Audrina's. If I paid for it, it's mine. I come from wig people. My grandmother Mary had wigs for going to church, visiting people in the hospital, and going shopping. Always topped off by a hat. I loved watching her carefully take her hair off the wig head and place it on her head, fixing it until it was just right.

I do it every day.

My grandmother was my good-luck charm. She had what appeared to be a direct line to God. I'd call her when I had a big audition.

"Grandma," I'd say, "I'm doing this comedy club and it's really important to me and I want to do well."

"All right," she'd say, getting ready to launch a barn-raising prayer that would surely propel me to stardom, or at least help me get my car back for the fifth, tenth, or fifteenth time.

"Lord," she'd say, introducing herself, "this is Your child, Mary Shepherd. I don't ask for much, Lord, but I'm coming to You for my grandbaby. I need my grandbaby to do well at the comedy club. I don't ask You for much, Lord, but I'm asking You for this."

Just in case the Lord's attention was elsewhere, Grandma would start crying and repeating.

"Just let my baby do *well*, Father! This is Your child, Mary Shepherd, and I don't ask for much!"

It's possible that the only reason the Lord put me on *The View* was to keep His child, Mary Shepherd, happy.

She lived in Chicago, and I regret that she only saw me perform once. I was going through a cursing phase. After my show at the Improv, Grandma gave me a talking-to.

"Sherri," she said, "you don't have to do all that dirty talking to make people laugh."

"I got to, Grandma!" I said. "Everybody does it." This was true. And it's nearly impossible to follow a very dirty act unless you also get dirty. I was always following dirty acts.

"You don't *have* to do it."

My dad gave me a similar lecture, which I ignored. When my grandmother passed away, I was struck by how many people came to her funeral so they could tell us what Mary Shepherd had done for them. She had prayed for them, too. I saw that life wasn't about the money. Grandma didn't have much, and what she did have was often sent to me, to help with rent and car repos.

My grandmother taught me that accomplishments meant less than what you left behind. I started to ask myself what impact my comedy could have on people's lives. And that changed my act. I got cleaner. I stopped talking about generic stuff like airplane peanuts and started speaking the truth about my life.

I tried doing road work, but after not getting paid, or getting left at a gig by the other comedian (who went home with a groupie), I decided to stay in Los Angeles. My agent couldn't send me on auditions if I was out of town.

> *So write yourself a permission slip to hark back to your dorky roots. Stop acting a fool, that ain't you, and you know it.**
>
> *As told by Mary Shepherd.

𝒩*ever lie to the wardrobe lady*

It was two years before I booked my first role. And it taught me an important lesson about lying. Don't do it to the wardrobe department. I was playing a maid on a *Candid Camera* type of show called *America's Totally Hidden Video*. The costume designer called, asking for my size.

"I'm a 10," I said.

I was a 16. At the shoot, the maid's uniform wouldn't even button across my chest. I ended up wearing my own tank top for my television debut.

Coinky-dink?

My next TV appearance had nothing to do with acting. I was the plaintiff's witness on a show called *Jones & Jury*. That's Jones as in Star Jones. My girlfriend was suing someone for taking her car. My job was, according to the show's producers, to be loud.

"Get mad," one said. "Shout!"

I did. "You *know* you took her car! You didn't return it!"

Miss Jones was not impressed. "Um, you need to be *quiet*," she said, as if she didn't know what the producers were telling me.

At one point she told me, "That's hearsay."

"It ain't hearsay!" I shouted. "I heard him say it and it's true!"

We lost the case.

One night, I had a set at the Laugh Factory. My agent had told me to call them, even though that club never worked me.

"There's gonna be people in the audience. Try to get a spot," she said.

I'd been trying to get spots there for years with no success, so why would today be any different?

It was. I'd called the club at the exact right time. "Actually, we have to fill an eleven thirty spot. Do you want it?"

Heck, yes.

Finally, some luck

It was more like midnight when I performed. The audience was tired but I had a great set anyway. The "people" in the audience included a man named Randy Stone, who was a development executive at Fox. Randy called me in for a meeting the next day, and just like that, I was given a fifty-thousand-dollar development deal.

A development deal meant that a Hollywood studio had just given me fifty grand to stay put while they tried to cast me in a sitcom. It was like getting an engagement ring from show business.

I was still working at the law firm. It was surreal. I'd have a lunch meeting at Fox, where Randy's assistants were asking me what temperature I preferred my water to be, and then I'd scramble back to work and get coffee and tea for the lawyers.

During my Fox meetings, I'd sneak looks at my watch, thinking, *I have to leave in ten minutes so I can file this brief by 2 PM.* At night, killing at comedy clubs, the audience howling. The next morning, late for work, get howled at. I was getting tension headaches, but I was too scared to quit.

"I can't leave, I need something stable," I complained to a boyfriend.

"Sherri," he said, "if it was all about stability, you wouldn't need faith."

> *So write yourself a permission slip*
> *to have some kind of faith—in God, in*
> *yourself. Then take a flying leap.*

Good-bye to all that

That was a thunderbolt moment. I realized that God gave me this special gift and I have to believe in it. My last day at the law firm was March 1. Nine days later, I was cast in Ellen Cleghorne's series for the WB, *Cleghorne!*

I spent every check as soon as I got it. And not on rent, but on my friends. On dinner. At clubs. I was so naive, I didn't know I had to give 10 percent of that money to my agency. And I didn't find out until I'd already spent it.

"What's commission?" I asked when they called. It was explained to me.

"Sorry," I said, "I'll pay you back."

Garrett Morris played Ellen's dad, and he looked out for me.

"Don't buy into the business," he said, gesturing to the set. "This set is here, but believe me, if this show gets canceled, they will break it down and it will be gone the next day."

Cleghorne! was canceled after one season. Now I was out of money, and I had no job. I didn't get another acting job for two years, and I returned to being a legal secretary. I was evicted, and my car was, yes, repoed.

Jungle years

I moved to a part of L.A. called The Jungle (54th and Crenshaw) and slept on a friend's couch. She was a comedian, too, and her day jobs were (a) phone sex operator, and (b) psychic hotline operator. She had calls coming in all day long.

"Hello, is Georgianne there?" someone would ask.

I'd hand the phone to Paula (her real name). The next thing I heard was either a prediction or a moan.

Paula's place in The Jungle was three bus rides from the law firm. But the final episodes of *Cleghorne!* were still airing, so people on the bus would recognize me.

"Aren't you on TV?"

"Yes."

"What are you doing on the bus?"

"Going to work."

Once I was eating a brown-bag lunch on a bench in Century City, and three Fox executives walked by. Just a few months ago, these guys had been offering me sandwiches and Evian. I hid, in case they recognized me, too.

I thought my career was over. A few years back, I'd appeared on an episode of *Friends*. Now I was temping at the same law firm where David Schwimmer's father was a partner. I was so afraid to buy anything that I wore the same outfit every day. And I still continued to take buses all over L.A. at night, doing comedy.

Finally, another break came when I was cast in a Scott Baio project. Good-bye, law. Three weeks before it was set to air, I got a call from the president of Warner Bros. Studios, Peter Roth.

"Sherri, I'm just sick to my stomach."

"No, don't tell me," I said.

He did anyway. Scott Baio's show was canceled. This hurt

even more because I'd turned down a recurring but smaller role on *Beverly Hills 90210* so I could take it. Hello, law.

A series regular!

Then I was hired as a regular on *Suddenly Susan*, Brooke Shields's show, which was already on the air and successful. Good-bye, law. I bought a house. On the day we were in escrow, I got a call from Brooke.

"Sherri," she said. Oh, no, I knew that tone. "We've been canceled."

I could not breathe. There would be no hello to law again, because this was not a legal secretary's house. This home is where you'd expect a cast member of a successful TV show to live, and I'd just bought it. There's no return to couch-surfing in The Jungle.

It turns out I was able make my house payments with residuals (the money you get paid when a TV show reruns) and stand-up gigs. I had enough name recognition from *Suddenly Susan* to make good money on the road.

The competition for parts can make it difficult to be friends with other actors. Brooke Shields and I got on great (and really, is there any competition for Brooke Shields?), but *Suddenly Susan*'s other female cast member and I did not. Now, I love Kathy Griffin, and she swears this didn't happen, but it did. My first few days on the set were like *Mean Girls*.

Kathy was *the* funny girl on the show. That was her thing. And then they brought in me, this black, sassy girl, to play Eric Idle's assistant. You'd think a skinny redhead who'd been in a Quentin Tarantino movie would have nothing to fear from me, but when the writers started giving me funny lines, Kathy got territorial. I was trespassing on her lawn. She decided to freeze me out.

I was just thrilled to be there, to be working again. One day, I was sitting in my dressing room and overheard Kathy planning lunch with the whole cast.

Yes, I was new, but I was part of the cast. Lunch day was approaching, and no one had asked me. I heard everyone walking down the hall.

"Where's Sherri?" asked Nestor Carbonell.

"Oh, she's gone," said Kathy.

I was crouched behind my door, thinking, *I'm not gone! I'm right here!*

I heard them all leave.

I curled up in my chair in a fetal position and *cried*. Snot was running out my nose. I was right back in high school during those awful moments when you're not in the clique, you're not picked for the team, and you're not asked to the dance . . . It was just awful.

I called Jeff.

"Kathy . . . lunch . . . Kathy . . . and . . . everyone . . . lunch . . . and . . . ," I blurted. I finally got it out.

"Sherri, there used to be one funny girl on *Suddenly Susan*," he said. "Now there's two."

A couple of weeks later, Kathy came over to me.

"You're really funny," she said.

From that moment on, we were inseparable. I think she just had to see that I was the real deal. And I just had to pick myself up and keep going. And trust that I was good enough at my job that everything would work out. And it did. Except for that "cancellation" thing.

Can you be five years younger?

Auditions were still tough. Once I was called back for a part to play a twenty-five-year-old. I was thirty. The producer called my agent.

"Everyone really likes Sherri, but it is imperative that when she comes back in for the network she looks twenty-five. Do whatever you can to make her look twenty-five."

I started calling everyone I knew.

"What are twenty-five-year-olds wearing these days?" I asked, as if I was a seventy-two-year-old grandpa trying to buy the right Christmas gift for his granddaughter.

"Go to Abercrombie and Fitch and get a pair of cargo pants," said a friend.

"Wear your hair in a ponytail," said another.

"Pink lip gloss, giant hoop earrings," said a third.

I showed up to the callback in a ponytail, cargo pants, and hoop earrings. Tempestt Bledsoe was in the waiting room. I'm competing against Vanessa Huxtable? When did she stop being ten?

My manager left a voice mail after the audition: "They went with someone else. They thought you looked too old."

I broke down in tears—not because I looked too old, but because I'd tried to look like someone else. If I'd gotten that part, I'd have shown up to work terrified every day that I was looking my age.

My next job was playing Jenny McCarthy's best friend, and my character was twenty-five. The hairstylist squinted at me.

"What can we do with your hair to make you look younger?"

"Nothing," I said. "Just put that curly wig on me and let's go!"

> **Write yourself a permission slip to stay true to yourself. If Barack Obama can keep his middle name, you can be your age.**

Dancing with DeGeneres

For a time, I was stuck in limbo. I didn't have enough acting credits to appear as a guest on shows like *Ellen, Regis and Kelly,* and *The View,* and I didn't have enough stand-up credits to appear on them as a comic. Living in L.A., I put all my energy into appearing on *Ellen.*

The producers kept saying no. They didn't know if I could sit on a couch and be funny. Like with my audition for Fox at the Laugh Factory, I got my chance when someone else canceled. My publicist happened to be on the phone with the *Ellen* people when that day's guest had to drop out.

"Can Sherri be here this afternoon?" the producer asked.

"She sure can," said my publicist.

When the band started playing the music, it was my cue to walk out. I noticed that none of the guests ever danced with Ellen, so I did.

"Come on, Ellen," I said, "bend over so I can pop your booty."

The appearance went well. Real well. I currently hold the record for the most appearances on *Ellen.* Betty White is second and Lauren Graham is third. I ended up with my own segment called

"The Shepherd Report," where I reported on pop culture. All from poppin' on Ellen's booty.

I flew myself out to New York so I could do *The Caroline Rhea Show*—I barely broke even on that deal.

Working on bed rest

I've always relied on the kindness of my female friends to help me get through the tough times. I was working on a show called *Less Than Perfect* when I got pregnant with Jeffrey. The executive producer of the show, Nina Wass, was also going through fertility treatments. I told her how scared I was of losing my job when I was on bed rest.

"Sherri," she said, taking my hand, "bringing this life into the world is more important than anything else. We'll do whatever you need. If you need us to write you out of the show—"

"No, don't do that!" I said.

I needed my Screen Actors Guild health insurance, and if I was written out of the show, I'd have no insurance during a high-risk pregnancy. The producers kept me on and made it easy by giving my character an "aww" or a "hey" on each episode.

On tape day, I would go into the studio in a wheelchair. I would carefully step out, say my "aww," then get back in the wheelchair and get rolled on home. (I'll be forever grateful to my good friends Niecy Nash, who's now on *Reno 911!*, and Yvette Nicole Brown, who's on *Drake & Josh*, for filling in for me at rehearsals.)

The doctors finally took me off bed rest. And that's when I got the call I'd been waiting for for three years: *The View*. I'd been trying and trying to get on the show.

In the circle of life, Johnnie Cochran passes me the baton

Johnnie Cochran died suddenly, and Star Jones would be out. (I guess you could say that my first appearance on *The View* was also due to a cancellation.) The producers called my agent.

"Can Sherri be in New York tomorrow?" they asked.

"She sure can," my agent said.

After that show, Joy Behar asked that I cover for her when she couldn't appear. And it took off from there.

To this day, I don't assume people recognize me. When I'm talking to audience members at *The View*, I introduce myself.

"I'm Sherri Shepherd."

"I know who you are!"

Never piss off a fan

Performers never get over their desire to be loved. In fact, at one point when I found out my husband was cheating, I called White J.Lo. In the middle of the argument, she said, "Sherri, I just have to tell you, you are so funny."

"Excuse me?" I asked.

"I have watched you. I'm such a fan."

"You know who I am?" I asked.

"I have followed your career for years," she said, "and I think you are so funny."

I should have gone off on her. I should have said, "Well, a real fan would show her appreciation by not having sex with my husband!"

Instead I said, "Thank you so much!"

You never want to lose a fan, even if she is sleeping with your husband. You never know when you're gonna need her to write a letter to the network saying, "Don't cancel Sherri Shepherd's show."

Dreams are contagious

I don't want to take anything for granted. I'm a walking testament that dreams can come true. And unlike bombing at a comedy club, dreams are contagious. Remember my friend Dianetta, the secretary who told me to go for it way back when? Well, after I got inspired by Dianetta, Dianetta got inspired by me.

She'd always wanted to be a real estate agent. So she quit the law firm, moved to Arizona, and got married. She earned her real estate license, and today she's one of the top agents in the state. Her billboard is on every major highway. A platinum-selling real estate agent. She tells me, "It's because of you, Sherri, that I decided to go past the fear and live my dream."

I've been a series regular on nine different television shows, which proves a cliché: When one door closes, another one opens. Then the cliché takes a turn, because that door closes and you're alone, in a locked room. But just as you're about to lose hope, a window opens. And closes behind you as soon as you crawl through it. Now you're outside. All the doors and windows to show business are locked, and you're wondering if you should quit. Then another door opens. But it's a trapdoor, and you have fallen into a pit. The trapdoor shuts, and you begin screaming, "Help! Help!" And that's when Barbara Walters calls and asks if you want to be a permanent co-host of *The View*.

It's so hard to see past the no's and believe that there's something better ahead. Just have yourself a good cry, put on your big-girl pants, and keep going. Someone will call you stubborn or single-minded. Maybe they're right, but we shouldn't have to apologize for it, justify it, or minimize it. Guys don't. So be ambitious and chase your dreams. But don't forget to pay your parking tickets. Armageddon's a long ways away.

I took my leap when my friend told me, "If it was all about stability, you wouldn't need faith." Your dreams might be different now than when you were a kid, but they're still there, waiting to be believed in.

> *So write yourself a permission slip to listen to that little voice in the back of your head, because it might not be so little.*

part four

Permission to Come Back to God

I talk to God, and He talks back. If you think I belong in a mental institution, well, you have something in common with Bill Maher.

God and I have always had a friendly, personal relationship, which surprises some people because I was raised in a strict religion. Being a Jehovah's Witness meant I had to adhere to rules that separated me from the rest of American culture. Witnesses don't celebrate birthdays or religious holidays. Christmas, for example, is a pagan holiday. But when I rebelled as a teenager, it was against the rules, not God.

Can I get a Witness?

The Witnesses refer to the place they worship every Sunday as the Kingdom Hall, not church. Nonbelievers attended church, we were told; Witnesses went to Kingdom Hall. When I was a teenager, I began participating in a tradition called role-playing. One Witness would pretend to be a nonbeliever (literally, like a devil's advocate). A second Witness would engage her in a mock debate about the faith. An example I remember is "standing in the teller's line at the bank."

This is how you were expected to handle a nonbeliever with whom you were acquainted:

Witness: "Hey, Jenny, how are you?"
Nonbeliever: "Oh, Sherri, I'm fine. I'm just feeling a bit
    depressed."
Witness: "Jenny, Jehovah doesn't want you to be depressed.
    Why don't we look at Psalm 183:18."

These little plays were watched by an audience of Witnesses, who would then critique our debate tactics. This exercise was to prepare us for field service on Saturday mornings.

Field service is, of course, when a Witness knocks on the front door and presents the faith to strangers, in their own homes. Like salesmen, Witnesses are trained to overcome your objections. Given the opportunity, a good Witness can rattle off eight Bible verses in under a minute. A door slammed in a Witness's face is seen as a challenge, not a rejection.

Questioning a faith

My dad started wavering from the faith when the church elders agreed with my mother. She wanted him to quit one of his jobs because it put him in close proximity to women. My dad was working as many jobs as necessary to feed a family of five, and when the elders took my mother's side, he began to doubt their wisdom. He started asking questions, which, if I remember my Reformation history correctly, doesn't go over well in rigid religious settings.

Ultimately, my father was "dis-fellowshipped"—which is like being excommunicated, but worse. After you've been dis-fellowshipped, Witnesses are not allowed to talk to you. If they see you on the street, they must look the other way. They cannot nod hello or look you in the eye. And since you are isolated from other people or cultures when you're in the church, after you're dis-fellowshipped, you are very alone. You have no one. Their hope is that you'll return to the flock out of sheer loneliness. Lots of people do. My dad wasn't one of them.

My sisters and I were told we had to separate ourselves from our father.

"You must tell him you can't talk to him anymore," said a church elder.

I couldn't do it. I worshipped my dad. And he was my *dad*, for gosh's sake. One of my favorite passages in the Bible is, "The greatest of these things is love, and you will know my followers by the love that they have."

How could I tell my own dad that I would never talk to him again? This man who sacrificed for us, who put cardboard in the soles of his shoes to cover up the holes, who bought school clothes for us on layaway at Kmart, who waited tables at Denny's and gave his tips to my sisters and me. How could my faith order me to turn my back on him?

I became disillusioned. The time after my parents' divorce was lonely, and the Jehovah's Witnesses were not a source of comfort. I started to rebel.

Looking back, I wonder if my mother wasn't bipolar at that time—or at the very least suffering from depression. She'd had several miscarriages and was in and out of the hospital. Her personality was so mercurial. In those days, no one really knew what clinical depression was—or how to treat it. At least no one in my circles. And the black community in particular was resistant to seeking therapy. Negative feelings were dirty laundry and you didn't air it. Perhaps the Witnesses gave my mom, who'd left her husband and moved with her three daughters to California, some solace and a sense of continuity.

But not me.

> *So write yourself a permission slip to question your elders. Just 'cause they're old doesn't mean they're smart.*

MJ keeps me in the faith, but not for long

As a teenager in Southern California, the most appealing thing about visiting the Kingdom Hall was the chance I'd run into Michael Jackson. He'd attend in disguise and sit privately in the library to listen to the Talks. MJ probably kept me religious for an extra six months.

I started to pull away. Lots of people do. I have a friend from eighth grade who's still a Witness. We vacation together. I'm sure people tell her not to associate with me. Once, we were hanging out and I noticed that she was drinking and swearing.

"Are you still in the church?" I asked.

"Oh yeah," she said, "I'm just taking a break. I'll go back in a minute, but right now I just need a little break."

I guess I'm still on a break—from the Witnesses, not God. I don't know if I was officially dis-fellowshipped; I never asked. Once I called an old friend to chat.

"Are you still going to the Kingdom Hall?" she asked immediately. It sounded like she knew what the answer would be.

"Oh no, I'm not a Jehovah's Witness anymore," I said.

She hung up.

Another friend I hadn't spoken to in over a decade also hung up on me. I had found her phone number. As soon as I told her who I was, her tone went cold.

"I haven't changed," I said. "I'm still the same person that you knew back then. I have the same sense of humor, I love to laugh. I have a child now and you have kids. It's me, Sherri."

Click. (I got an e-mail from her after I joined *The View*. I did not reply.)

Godtalk

My faith means everything to me. God and I talk constantly. Of course, I don't always do what God tells me to do. Because every now and then, I think my ideas are better than God's.

My parents taught me that no problem is too big or small for God. The notion of prayer brings to mind kneeling in a Sunday outfit at church, murmuring the Lord's Prayer, but for me it can be much simpler.

Lord, can You find me a parking space nearby, 'cause I cannot walk nine blocks in these heels.

God doesn't always find me a good parking space, but I'm not afraid to ask. I'm pushy that way.

I ask Him to intervene on the big stuff. My son was hospitalized for several months after his birth; it was touch-and-go for a while. Even after he was out of mortal danger, Jeffrey remained in intensive care, with tubes going in and out of his body.

One day, I couldn't take much more. I often prayed for my son, but now I was worried for myself. I couldn't imagine going back to stand-up comedy. Nothing was funny anymore, and I didn't know how I'd make a living or take care of this baby when he came home.

God, I can't even smile, much less tell a joke. How are we gonna survive?

"You will," God said. "Just trust in Me and know that I'm going to take care of this boy."

He did.

Another time, I lay in bed next to the person who had betrayed me. I prayed.

How can I go on? I feel like I want to die.

And I heard God's voice, telling me, "You will make it through this, just trust in Me."

I did.

After I moved to New York, my son stayed in L.A. I would sit in my apartment and look at pictures of me holding Jeffrey. And then look at my empty arms. And again, God would soothe me, ask me to trust in Him.

My son lives with me now.

I have to rely on God. I can't even binge on food anymore

because I have diabetes. I'd ask God why I couldn't zone out and have some cheesecake, like everyone else. And that voice, again, "You will get through this if you just trust in Me."

I have, so far.

God sounds like Barry White

I can see why people like Bill Maher fear us "Godtalkers." Some of us hear some scary stuff. George Bush said he talked to God, too, but according to George, they discussed war. Maybe George misheard. In all the conversations I've had with God, He never once told me to invade Iraq.

In fact, my God-voice sounds like a guy straight outta *Shaft*. He speaks in a deeply masculine voice that is comforting and authoritative at the same time.

> *So write yourself a permission slip to talk to God. Just don't freak out if He talks back. And don't say "You sound just like Barry White!" He prefers "Barry White sounds just like You!"*

God gives me the creeps and I obey, sort of

When I was in my late teens, I was doing a dumb thing (surprise) in L.A.—hitchhiking. Because the bus took so long, sometimes men would drive by and ask if I needed a ride. Sleep-deprived, broke, and constantly late for legal secretary school—I often said yes.

One time a guy pulled up, and said, "Do you need a ride?" I must have had a suspicious look on my face, because he added, "I'm not crazy. I'm not one of those guys that's gonna kill you."

Which meant that he probably was. In retrospect this is so obvious. Why would you bring up something you're *not* gonna do when you meet someone?

"Hi, I'm Sherri and I'm not gonna break into your house when you're on vacation."

"Uh, okay?"

I got in the car. He did get me to school without killing me, but I always wonder if there was a chain saw in his trunk. That guy gave me "preliminary willies." God was using him to plant the seed of wariness I would need during another ride a few months later. The next driver was a white, bald guy. Kinda looked like Joe the Plumber. He was taking me to school. It was a fifteen-minute drive, and he started talking.

"Have you ever been to a toga party?"

"What's a toga?" I asked. I was a young eighteen.

"People wear sheets. And they don't wear anything under their sheets."

Whoa. God struck me with an urge to open the door and roll out of a moving car. I didn't know if the man was taking me to a sex party, or if this was just my normal apprehension when a white guy talks about wearing sheets. Either way, I wanted out. I remained silent, praying for help.

"Have you ever seen a snuff film?" he asked.

"I don't even know what a snuff film is."

"It's where people are watching other people have sex. They're fun. Are you sure you've never seen one?"

"I'm sure."

"Would you like to see one?"

"No. I have to be at class." I noticed that the knob to unlock the door was missing. I was locked in. I began looking for an opportunity to jump. A stoplight, *please turn red*. I started sobbing. This ride was turning into one of those *Cosmo* fiction stories.

"Let me out please," I said.

Thank God he did. I guess I ruined his vibe. Later I found out that people die in snuff films. Hence the term *snuff*.

So you're probably thinking I stopped hitching rides right after that. Oh, you're not? You know me by now? Okay, then you know that I kept on hitching for about six more months. Finally, my girlfriend Earlene said, "Girl, what on earth are you doing? You could get killed!"

She got through to me. I needed to have someone else say it. My own feelings weren't enough proof.

> *So write yourself a permission slip to respect the willies, the creeps, or whatever you call them. That's God's way of saying, "Get out now!"*

Panhandled by an angel

I believe in angels. I've seen several of them. If you think you've never seen an angel, maybe it's because you're looking for a Gerber baby with wings, or Jaclyn Smith. *None* of my angels ever looked like that. In fact, most of Sherri's Angels were in need of a long, soapy bath and a new pair of shoes.

One night, back in my open-mic days, I was waiting for the bus home to downtown L.A. from Igby's in West L.A. It was 1 AM. Instead of running every half hour, the bus was running every hour.

I was in my comedy outfit—thigh-high boots and a mini. At a bus stop after midnight, of course, I didn't look like I was out telling jokes.

A few guys appeared in two nearby doorways, whispering to me.

"Psst," said one man.

I peered down the street, looking for the lumbering headlights of that damn bus. Nothing.

"Psst . . . hey," said another shadow.

I was terrified. More than an hour had passed by without a bus. I had no money for a cab. It was too late to wake anybody up and ask for a lift. *Where is that damn bus?*

A homeless black man sat down on the bench next to me. He seemed harmless. I made nervous conversation with him. I felt a little safer, but not much.

A car started driving around and around, circling me. The driver kept propositioning me, and getting angrier and angrier as I ignored him.

I kept up the chatter with the homeless man, and kept looking for that bus. Did the bus driver fall asleep or something? The car circled again, then stopped in front of the bench. The windows were rolled down, and the driver was swearing at me. My heart was pounding. The homeless man leapt off the bench and leaned into the car window.

"Listen," he said, "if you come back again, I'm going to blow your head off."

The homeless man sat back down next to me, protectively. The car took off and did not return. I was still terrified, but clearly this homeless guy meant me no harm. We began to talk about God. More minutes passed, and finally, finally, the wide-set headlights of a city bus ambled their way toward my stop.

"Can I give you some money?" I asked the homeless man, even though I had almost none.

"No," he said. He must've known. Who would take the bus home if they had money?

"I stabbed a man two weeks ago," he said.

I stared at him. He wasn't bragging or trying to scare me. Just statin' a fact.

"Don't be taking the bus this late at night," he warned. "You don't need to be doing this."

The bus doors opened. I hugged him before I stepped up. On the long ride home, it occurred to me that God had sent an angel to protect me during that dangerous hour, and the angel was an old black homeless man who'd just stabbed someone. You might be asking, *Why didn't God just send the bus a little earlier?* I can't speculate, but I do know that ever since that night, I've never judged a homeless person.

Cutting through the park

Having said that, I haven't always learned my lesson as quickly as I could have. Luckily God is persistent. I used to cut through MacArthur Park to go home. The closest bus stop was a thirty-minute walk from where I lived. Although the park was extremely dangerous, walking through it saved me twenty minutes.

Naive? Yes, but I was from the 'burbs. That's how we do.

I've since decided that two types of suburban girls move to the rough part of town. One is the kind who doesn't realize she's *in* a bad part of town until after the landlord cashes the security deposit and it's too late. She usually moves as soon as the lease is up. That was not me. The other type is the girl who thinks bad things won't happen to her because bad things haven't happened to her. Yet.

That was me.

I thought I was invincible. I'd walk through MacArthur Park with my "mean mug" on. I was trying to look intimidating to muggers and rapists, but I was five foot one, wearing boots I couldn't run in and a halter top that anyone could yank off in a second. I probably looked pissed off that my feet hurt.

God would generally put in His two cents as I approached the entrance to the park, narrowing my eyes in a menacing fashion.

"Don't go through that park," God would say, sternly. "Walk around, Sherri, walk around."

"It saves me twenty minutes, and I'm so tired!" I'd say.

Night after night, I survived my shortcut. God's warnings began to lose their power, like the boy crying wolf. One night, I again blew God's advice off and headed in.

A homeless man jumped out of nowhere and started screaming at me.

"Only three kinds of people go through this park," he shouted.

"Homeless people, drug addicts, and hookers. And you not none of them!"

I began to walk faster, my mean mug collapsing and melting into a face of sheer terror. He followed me, shouting over and over.

"You're not none of 'em! I don't want to see you in this park no more!"

I ran. I ran in boots I couldn't run in and didn't stop until I was home. Had he been watching me for weeks and finally decided to say something? I don't know, but that was my last cut-through. The very next week, a woman was raped in MacArthur Park.

Saved by a second homeless angel. Later, my grandmother Mary told me she'd been praying extra hard that week.

"Baby, I just felt something," she told me. "I felt something. I had been praying for you strong this week."

"Don't go in that park."

Some people call that voice intuition, but I call it God. And whenever I pat God on the head and go on my own way, that's when trouble comes. God warned me about Terry; I ignored Him. God asked me to forgive my husband. I'm not in a place of complete forgiveness yet, but my husband is still alive, and believe me, that was all God's doing.

God and I have a disagreement, He wins

I have debated God. Early in our marriage, my husband was trying to create a budget. I had a habit of buying whatever I wanted (Armageddon being around the corner and all), and the constant money crunch was harming our marriage. We agreed that if I wanted to buy anything over a hundred dollars, I would call Jeff first. Actually, it went both ways, but I was the only one making large purchases, so the rule was really directed at me.

A DSW Shoe Warehouse had opened near our home. DSW sells designer shoes at discount prices, and if I sound like an evangelist, it's because I am. Gucci shoes with a Marshall's price tag. Now, it's possible I was in a shoe-induced haze, but I could swear I heard God talking to me.

"Sherri, I want you to have nice shoes, and that's why I brought this DSW Warehouse to your neighborhood."

"You don't say!" I said, grabbing my checkbook and the car keys.

"Yes," God continued. His voice sounded a little higher than usual, less Barry White's and more . . . mine. But I paid it no mind. Maybe God had a cold. "Sherri, I'd like you to go *right now* and shoe those little feet of yours, those feet that I lovingly handcrafted on the day you were born."

"All right, God," I said, nearly running a stop sign. "If You say so!"

At DSW, surrounded by shoes and armed with a joint checking account, I worshipped God by bringing $189 worth of merchandise to the cashier. As I wrote the check, God piped up.

"Jeff told you anything over a hundred dollars, you need to discuss it with him."

God was sounding more like His old Self. Hmm. I guess God can get over a cold in a few minutes, but I still had a hard time believing this was the same Lord who had just told me to hightail it to the store and buy shoes.

"God, don't take this wrong, but are you sure that's You?"

"You were supposed to call him," God said, sternly. Shoot. That sure sounded like Him.

One of my favorite Bible stories is the tale of Gideon and the fleece. Basically, God wanted Gideon to lead the Israelites into battle, and Gideon didn't want to unless God promised the Israel-ites would win. Gideon wanted a sign from God. Gideon told an angel that he would leave a fleece out overnight. If he woke up the next morning and the fleece was wet but the ground was dry, that would be the sign that the Israelites would win.

Gideon put the fleece out and went to sleep. When he woke up the next morning, the fleece was wet and the ground dry. But Gideon was still worried, so he asked God for a second, reverse sign—that he would wake up the next morning and find the fleece dry but the ground wet. God, I assume, rolled His eyes and said, "Okay." Gideon awoke the next morning to find the fleece dry and the ground wet. Gideon led the Israelites into battle and to victory.

"God," I said, "if Gideon can ask for a sign, can I?"

I didn't hear a no, so I laid out the details of my potential surrender.

"Lord, if this is You talking to me, You see that I'm about to write out this check. If, as I write out this check, my checkbook gets wet, then I know You don't want me to buy these shoes. If the checkbook stays dry before I sign my name," I said, writing as fast as I could, "then this is a sign I'm supposed to buy these shoes."

I often pray in silence, but this time I was praying out loud. I didn't care who heard; I was having an important discussion with the Lord regarding matters of commerce.

"I don't hear anything, Lord," I said.

Now, I'm not the type of person who spits when I talk. We all know people like this and we stand far from them when they speak. I'm not one of them. Not even the occasional drop flies out of my mouth. Well, as I was praying and signing the *Shep* part of *Shepherd,* a tiny drop of spittle sailed out of my mouth and landed on the check.

"No!" I said, looking at my wet checkbook.

The drop landed on the top left corner, on the address where I lived with my husband, who would surely appreciate a phone call right about now.

"You think you're funny now, too?" I asked God. He did not reply, but the drop began to sink into the paper, turning into a spot that was staring me down.

"Sorry, God, but that's a coincidence, not a sign," I said.

I put my thumb over the spit spot, finished signing my name, and bought the shoes.

My plan was to leave them in my closet for a few weeks. I couldn't wear them immediately, because Jeff would notice. I schemed to unroll them slowly, one pair a month. If Jeff asked, I'd say I'd always had them.

But God kept nagging me.

"Sherri, you were wrong. You agreed to abide by that rule and you didn't."

"God, why can't You look at that purchase as two small purchases that were combined?" I asked. "One for ninety dollars, and one for ninety-nine dollars. And I conserved paper by adding them together and writing out just one check for $189!"

God wasn't buying what I was selling.

I waited a few weeks, then went to the closet. Today, I told myself, I would try to sneak the Guccis by Jeff. I pulled out the shoes, and one of the c's had fallen off the shoes. It was nowhere to be found. Now my "designer" shoes were by GU CI.

I never wore them. To me, it was a sign that *coincidence* starts with a *c* and the *c* dropped off my shoe. God won that one, too.

Pinkberry . . . Satan's franchise?

Sometimes I wonder: If it wasn't God who put the DSW Shoe Warehouse in my neighborhood, who was it? And is it the same entity that put a Pinkberry within walking distance of my apartment in New York?

Pinkberry is a yogurt shop—maybe it's just in L.A. and New York. Think of it as meth. Once you start, you'll be unable to stop. And food is my drug. I am a food addict, and the best food on earth is five minutes away from my apartment on foot. (Thirty seconds by cab.) The temptation was so great I practically had to pull God away from His work with the poor and hungry just to deal with my bingeing.

When I first moved to New York to start *The View*, I was alone. My son was in Los Angeles, as were my friends and family. I was afraid every day on set would be my last, and I was full of anxiety.

Then along came Pinkberry.

One spoonful of green tea yogurt turned me into a three-times-per-day user. Diabetics like me are supposed to have thirty grams of sugar and thirty grams of carbs per day max, and one serving of Pinkberry had thirty-three grams of each. And because I was spending so much time at the shop, the staff began to top off my large cups. Making them into extra-larges, super-extra-larges, and something they should just call Sherri-size. And then I started getting a medium "on the side." A Sherri-size green tea, and a medium vanilla. With bananas.

I told myself I was getting fruit and dairy, but really I was eating at least four times the amount of carbs and sugar that my body could handle. And it wasn't about gaining weight, it was about staying alive. My mother died at age forty-one from complications due to diabetes, and here I was, approaching that exact age, with suicidal eating habits. Diabetes kills Shepherds and yet I couldn't stop.

Forgetting the definition of Anonymous

I'd always had a food obsession. People in my family have addictive, compulsive personalities. I don't drink because I'm afraid I'll accidentally trigger my inner alcoholic. When I lived in L.A., I attended some 12-step meetings for food addiction. I saw a famous sitcom actor at one of those meetings. One time I said, "Hi, I'm Sherri S., and I'm such a fan!"

A friend pulled me aside and said, "We don't do that at Anonymous meetings."

I was a plump teen, but never fat. When I was doing open mics in L.A., my mom was in the hospital and my boyfriend was in prison. I dove into food right around then. The spiritual side of the 12-step meetings gave me some peace around my food issues. After I moved to New York, I got so caught up in the show, the divorce, and my son that I experienced some backsliding on the food.

The sugar high helped me dull the pain from the custody battle. Every weekend, flying back to L.A. to be with my son, I'd stop by Pinkberry and get two servings. I'd eat one in the cab, and let the other one melt so I could drink it at the airport.

God slays Pinkberry

I knew I was killing myself. One day, I made an announcement on *The View* that I had to stop. Yet right after the show, I was headed to Pinkberry. I was about twenty feet from the store when God spoke, loud and clear.

"NO MORE PINKBERRY. NO MORE PINKBERRY."

I had never heard God thunder before. I'd read about such tremblings in the Bible, but in all the conversations I'd had with God over the years, He'd never made me cower. Not when I was headed into MacArthur Park, not when I was about to bash Jeff's skull in. But as I approached this little yogurt shop, God thundered.

"NO MORE PINKBERRY. NO MORE PINKBERRY."

This was not the loving advice of a New Testament God. This was the fearsome booming command of an Old Testament God. This was the God who drowned every creature on earth save the passengers on Noah's boat. This was the God who killed every firstborn Egyptian boy on Passover, and this God, well, He wanted me to stay the heck out of Pinkberry.

I haven't been back since.

> **So write yourself a permission slip to
> ask God to help you slay your Pinkberry.**

Finally choosing Him

I believe that God leaves you with a spiritual hole that He wants you to fill with Him. But He also gives you free will—and that's the stuff that got me in trouble. In my twenties, I filled that hole with food, shopping, and sex. I was pregnant numerous times, I had many abortions. I was twenty-five thousand dollars in credit card debt.

Long Beach, in California, used to be a dangerous town. I would perform at a club there, then I'd park my car someplace and sit. I thought, *If somebody came and killed me right now, I wouldn't matter. Life would just go on.*

One night, I just broke down. I was having one of those girl-cries. When your body is shaking, your stomach muscles hurt from clenching, and your room is cluttered with snot balls. I was on my knees, and my silent treatment to God ended.

"Lord," I said, "if You care for me at all. If I matter to You at all, can You show me what I'm supposed to do? Something, please!"

I didn't get an answer. Not from Barry White, not even from that other "God" who sounds like me and tells me to buy shoes. But all of a sudden, people started entering my life and praying with me. And that gave me a new peace.

Lydia was an actress and a comedian. Like me, she hung out at The Comedy Store, hoping for a spot. Shortly after I fell to my knees, Lydia approached me at the Store and took my hands.

"God told me there's a heaviness, you got a burden around you. And I got to pray with you."

Well, I didn't really appreciate that, especially since we were trying to be taken seriously at a comedy club. And Lydia prayed loudly. She is a dear friend now, and when we go out to dinner, she doesn't settle for a mumbled Lord's Prayer. She will make all participants grab hands and start preaching at the table—for ten or fifteen minutes. When she finishes and you look up, half the restaurant is staring at you. But I guess that's what I needed. Lydia would call me at six in the morning: "I want to pray with you."

It helped.

Many times, strangers would stop me and say, "How are you?" Especially on the bus, during my many trips and transfers, someone would sit next to me, ask how I was doing, and we'd end up in a conversation about God.

Those moments saved me.

> *So write yourself a permission slip to let God work through a stranger. Some of those folks really know their stuff.*

The angel who borrowed ten dollars

I try to return the spiritual favor now that I'm in a better place. Once, I was in the subway and a homeless woman stepped into my car. In New York, homeless people can shout their entire tale of woe in the time it takes the train to travel ten city blocks—less than a minute. I'm always a sucker for a good story.

This lady cleared her throat and began.

"Ladies and gentlemen! My home burned to the ground. I have two children and a disabled husband, who is blind." People were looking away, but she continued.

"We are living in a hotel room that the Red Cross has provided.

But they can do no more. I am a hardworking woman. I don't beg. But I find myself in this predicament."

The train reached the next stop. At this point, most homeless people get whatever money they can and hop into a new car. But she stayed with us.

"I just ask if you would search your heart and see if you can help me and my disabled husband who is *blind* and my two children."

I'm not proud to say that I was annoyed with her persistence. Not making any judgments, but her life circumstances were preventing me from losing myself in a romance novel. And after a hundred pages of foreplay, the main characters were about to have sex, so I needed this gal to put a cork in it.

Then I heard a voice.

"Go give her ten dollars."

Guess who?

"Ten dollars!" I said. "Lord, I know You're talking to me, but can't I just give that girl a dollar? Ten dollars is a lot!"

"Give her ten dollars," God said.

"I can't. I only got eleven on me. I'm gonna give her ten and leave me with one?"

"Sherri!" God said. He was not having any of it.

I folded over the corner of page 101 so I wouldn't lose my place, stood up, and gave her a ten-dollar bill.

"I hope to God you are telling the truth," I said. "If your blind husband and your kids are in the hotel, then it's okay. Please be telling the truth because I'm giving you my money."

"Thank you," she said. And then she asked me to bow my head so she could pray for me. I did, but I was chewing out God under my breath.

"Look, Lord, if You wanted to comfort me, why do You have to do it through this crazy lady? Why can't You do it at church, where the preacher says, 'Hey, Sherri, get on up here so we can pray with you!' Why can't You do it that way, Lord?"

God did not respond. However, as soon as I got off the train, my depression was lifted.

My only complaint is that God keeps speaking to me through homeless people. It's getting a little repetitive. Just once, can't George Clooney or Blair Underwood teach me a lesson? In fact, Lord, if You're reading this, if Blair were to take my hands and ask me to pray with him, I promise You, whatever lesson I was supposed to learn that day, I would learn *forever*.

I'm not complaining. I'm just a single mom who wouldn't mind being saved by an angel over six feet tall with a film credit.

> *Write yourself a permission slip to*
> *find grace in the ungraceful places.*
> *Clooney is coming, I promise.*

Risking hellfire and damnation

I was saved in 1993. Someone suggested I try a Pentecostal church. Now, recall that I grew up believing that a Jehovah's Witness does not set foot in church. Witnesses are Christian, but they don't believe a lot of the same things Christians do, or participate in the same rituals. The idea of a Holy Trinity—that Jesus and God and the Holy Ghost were Three and One—just didn't add up at Kingdom Hall. Witnesses also don't believe in Hell. Wicked souls are annihilated, and that's that.

When I stepped in this church, I was overcome with a fear of Wrath. Capital W, old-school biblical Wrath. With each step I took forward, I wondered if everything behind me would explode, like some kind of Damien movie.

I sat in the last row, as a service to everyone in front of me.

A preacher was preaching. This was a black Pentecostal church. If you've never been, it's hard to describe the mayhem. Parishioners in ecstasy, running up and down the aisles, spouting gibberish.

I was shocked. I'd never seen this kind of emotion at the Kingdom Hall. Witnesses are extremely orderly and polite. They sing, with songbooks, "From house to house. From door to door. Jehovah's word we spread." They play the piano. They stand, they sit, stand and sit. No one runs down the aisle, not even if they have a bathroom emergency.

But these Pentecostals! Howling because they got the Holy Ghost inside them. The ladies wearing hats as large as fruit baskets. Singing—no, screaming—"Hallelujah!" And everyone with hands raised to the sky, speaking in a nonsense language that sounded like a poor man's Spanish but was, of course, *tongues.*

It was like being raised on Enya and then stumbling into a James Brown concert. *What the heck have I walked into?* I asked myself.

I loved it.

Within minutes, I was overcome with a profound sense of peace. The chaos made me feel calm. I belonged there.

> *So write yourself a permission slip
> to surrender, to something, just once
> in your life. Of course, it's none of my
> business what that thing is. And if it's
> not God, I hope he's at least cute.*

Andy Dick, assignment from God

Andy Dick came to my church.

Okay, let me backtrack. I'm not a preacher, I don't tell you how to live your life or judge you. But if we get to talking, I may mention how amazing my relationship with God is. I feel like no matter where you go, somebody's supposed to be touched by you. My love for God should show in how I conduct myself. My hope is that you'll notice I'm different, and ask me what my secret is.

Andy holds a special place in my heart now; he's like my second baby. However, when I was first cast opposite Andy on *Less Than Perfect*, the thought of even meeting him terrified me.

"This boy, Andy Dick, who's on the show, is crazy. He's bisexual, he wears cocktail dresses. *E! True Hollywood* did a *Story* on him!" I told a girlfriend.

"You don't even know him," she said. She prayed with me a lot, so she wasn't having any of my fear. "Maybe that's someone God wants you to love on. Maybe Andy Dick is an assignment from God."

"God ain't told me nothing," I said. "I ain't heard no voice, I didn't get no assignment, no homework, nothing. If Andy Dick is my project, God sure hasn't told me yet."

We were taping the pilot (the first episode). To my delight, Andy and I had hit it off.

"I'm so glad you got the job," he said the first time we met.

His energy was crazy—kind of Pentecostal, now that I think of it. (Of course his *actions* weren't Pentecostal, but I haven't given up on Andy yet.)

One day, Andy walked up to me. He looked sad.

"Sherri, can God love someone like me?"

He started crying. He put his head in my chest and I held him. I was so ashamed of how I'd judged him. God was telling me, "He needs Me, too, Sherri. You ain't the only one who wants a parking space."

We talked about God. Even now, Andy will call me in the middle of the night for a pick-him-up. He's usually unaware of the time.

"Sherri, how are you?" he'll say softly. We'll talk God and comedy and God and love. I usually end the call with a short prayer.

"Lord, Andy is such a tortured soul. And I just hope and pray that he gets it together. Before it's too late. 'Cause inside there's this little kid who just is lost and who hasn't been treated so nicely. And this kid acts out and is very brilliant."

Sometimes, I get a different kind of "Andy" call.

"Sher-eeeeeeeeeeeeeeeeeeeee!"

That banshee call is my cue to cradle the phone between my ear and my neck so I can raise my hands and start prayin', loud.

Once, during my fertility treatments, I got a "Sher-eeeeeeeeeeeeee" call. I was supposed to be lying down with my legs in the air so this sperm and egg could meet, fall in love, and implant themselves in my uterine lining, but Andy had just fallen off the wagon.

"Sher-eeeeee! I need you, I need you to come."

I decided that this sperm and egg would have to drift in utero for a few more hours, because my baby Andy needed me. I rolled off the bed and drove to his house. I held my crotch the whole way over, as if I could keep the egg inside with my hand. I found Andy sitting in his underwear, very upset.

We prayed. That particular sperm–egg combo did not take, but as long as I'm alive, I'll be praying over Andy Dick.

He called me while he was taping the show *Celebrity Rehab*.

"Hey how you doing?" he asked, sober.

"I'm good, where you at?"

"I'm in rehab," he said.

"Huh? How do you call me from rehab? Aren't you sequestered?"

Andy asked if I could come to him and pray with him, without mentioning that our prayers would be taped for the television show. I said yes. I started rearranging my flight schedules. I mentioned it to a friend.

"Oh, you gonna be on TV?"

"Uh, no."

"Sherri, they're bringing a camera crew, to film you praying with Andy Dick."

I couldn't do it. Prayer is a very personal thing to me. I can share my faith in private or on the phone, but praying on TV is not me. I don't want to pour my heart out to God and then be followed by a Viagra commercial.

But I was willing to bring Andy Dick to my Pentecostal church. Andy had been pestering me for a while, but never committing to a time. Finally, I nailed down a Sunday and he agreed.

"Church starts at eleven, Andy," I said on Saturday afternoon. "I'm picking you up at ten thirty."

He called me at 10 AM on Sunday.

"I just want to make sure you're coming, Sher-eeee."

Uh-oh. I didn't like the sound of that *Sherri*. Too many e's.

"Andy, I'm on my way," I said, worried.

When I got to his house, Andy was surrounded by at least six bodyguards. Or just huge friends. It looked and smelled like they had just gotten back from a nightclub. Like, minutes ago.

We piled like clowns into two cars.

"I didn't expect all this," I told Andy, motioning to the car behind us. "But you know, hey, the more the merrier."

Andy brought a big bowl of gumballs. Huge. About a thousand gumballs. Enough to keep you chewing through a nuclear winter.

"I bought this for the kids in Sunday school. The little kids," he explained.

I didn't have the heart to tell him that most parents would wonder why Andy Dick was giving their children gumballs. We pulled into the parking lot. Lots of women were walking into church.

"The women here are so fuckin' hot!!!" shouted Andy.

Uh-oh.

"Andy," I said, "you can't be cursing when we going to church!"

A pretty blonde walked by.

"She is fucking hot!" said Andy.

"Andy, that's the pastor's wife!" I said. "You're going to get swallowed up into the ground right now. And I'm going with you 'cause you're in my car!"

He kept commenting on various Pentecostal body parts. I was freaking out.

"Andy, this is Sunday. I'm coming here with you. You smell like booze," I said. I looked at his six friends. "I don't know who all these dudes are. Everybody here is dressed up and y'all look like a bunch of ragtag punk rockers!"

"Oh Sher-eeeeee."

Andy dropped off his gumballs at the nursery school. The kids got very excited. He passed them out like Santa. The teacher let Andy Claus work his magic; she could see how excited he was to be making kids happy. At the service, the usher found seats for all eight of us. Yes, Andy was loud, but so were the Pentecostals, and neither of them seemed to mind the other.

> *Write yourself a permission slip to be surprised by someone's potential. Who knows, one day that person could be you.*

A new woman

When you're born again, it's like you're a new person. The old person is gone. The way you think and conduct your life is different.

I am a Christian, but I haven't been baptized or dunked in a river. One of these days, I may just saunter on over to the Hudson and make it official. But I feel legit. God often asks me to perform a service as I'm walking on the street.

"Sherri, I need you to pray with that person."

I always try. Many times I have approached total strangers and asked, "Do you mind if I pray with you?"

If they say they do, I move on. But mostly, God sends me to people who say yes. I'm so grateful for Lydia, who took my hand when I was so low and asked, "Can I pray with you?" I want to repay the favor, as many times as I can.

Thanks, Big Guy

Often, God calls to me in the middle of the night.

"Come talk to Me," He says. Sometimes God seems as lonely as me. I will curl up in a rocking chair at 4 AM and look up at the dark, silent sky and over to the son I thought I would never have.

"Thank You," I say. A lot of my praying is just saying thanks.

"Thank You for my son, thank You for my job."

When I ask for "things," it's usually wisdom or guidance. I worry about my sister, who has five kids and all the angst that comes with them. I ask God to help her be strong.

My role on *The View* has inspired hours of praying. Sometimes I cannot believe this turn my life has taken. I am a stand-up comic. I'm an actress. Give me lines, and I will make them funny. But to be asked my opinion, every day, is still overwhelming to me. Growing up as a Witness, my family didn't discuss politics at the dinner table. Every day, I ask God to give me some wisdom, help me contribute *something* to this conversation.

My bills get paid on time. I don't have credit problems. I have a new set of problems, but because of my relationship with God, I always have hope. I *never* had hope before. Just a depressing, bleak heaviness. A blackness. When I started talking to God, going to church . . . it was like someone flipped on the lights in my tunnel.

God and the city

I've been trying to find a church in New York City. I took the A train to Harlem and saw a couple standing on the street. They looked holy enough to me.

"Do you know where a good church is?" I asked.

"Oh, yes, go to the Holy Mount Choir," said the woman. She seemed very excited, and pointed me in the right direction. (I changed the name of this church so I don't hurt anyone's feelings.)

Now, I always thought my Pentecostal church in Los Angeles was intense, but it doesn't hold a candle to the Holy Mount Choir. The worship was loud. Drums started beating and a woman ran up the aisle, crying out in tongues. I thought, *How did you get the Holy Ghost so fast? You just came out of the bathroom! Don't you have to sing a little?*

Then the pastor began his sermon.

"And the Lord said, 'Out!'" he shouted, which I thought was a little bizarre. If you start the sermon with a yell, where do you go from there? Screaming? Setting your hair on fire? I was being kind of quiet. The pastor looked at me and said, "If you don't praise the Lord, He's gonna take your joy!"

That made me mad. I have joy, I just don't feel like shouting about it. An old woman who probably prayed with Abraham himself elbowed me.

"You better praise the Lord," she said. I was afraid she'd hit me with her cane if I didn't.

I got talked into inviting two of the older ladies to my apartment, so they could bless it. They brought Holy Oil that they said was from Israel. I noticed that the bottle said MADE ON CRENSHAW, but who am I to burst anyone's bubble?

They began walking around my apartment, shouting. I followed.

"In the name of Jesus, we bind up that spirit of worry," said one woman.

"Go on, get out worry!" I said.

"In the name of Jesus, we bind up that spirit of fear," said the other.

"Go on, get out fear!" I said. I was feeling better already.

"In the name of Jesus, we bind up that spirit of lust and desire!"

I did not repeat. Instead, I prayed silently that they would go on and leave my apartment. I'm still looking for a church. Despite their best efforts, every day I worry about my son, fear the economy, and lust for the right man or Pinkberry.

God gets radical to save my life

People think I'm really crazy when I tell them that diabetes has saved my life.

Most people, including my sister, get the diagnosis and become depressed. But it was such a big wake-up call for me. It was God saying, "For years and years, Sherri, I've been telling you not to fill that hole in your heart with those M&M's and cake, but you never listened. It's time to listen."

Diabetes has forced me to rethink everything that I put into my mouth. Without this disease, I would have reacted to the stress of moving to New York by overeating. But when you numb your feelings with food, you miss out on life, in its rawest form.

So many Christians say to me, "Pray to the Lord that He delivers you from that diabetes! I'm going to pray that He just take the diabetes away!"

"Don't pray for that," I say. "It keeps me honest. Diabetes is like checks and balances for my spiritual constitution."

The worst thing a doctor could tell me would be, "Sherri, you are diabetes free, you can eat whatever you want."

Before he even finished the sentence, I'd be on the sidewalk, hailing a cab and heading straight to the IHOP on 135th Street. I'd order a full stack of pancakes, with bacon, strawberry syrup (mixed with old-fashioned maple syrup), fried eggs, and toast with a lot of butter. Steamed vegetables would be a thing of the past.

You would never see me again. I'd call in sick to *The View* and keep ordering short stacks (IHOP is open 24/7) until I grew too large to leave the booth. Eventually I'd lose my job, my apartment, and my son. So I never ask God to cure me of diabetes. Instead, I ask for the strength to order steamed vegetables when everyone else is having french fries.

Sometimes, I'll ask God to keep me around for a special occasion.

"God, can I see my son walk down the aisle? And if You are in a good mood, can I see my grandbabies, too? But I'd like to not be in a wheelchair. And I'd like to have both my feet. Please just let me see my baby walk down the aisle, and let me look down and see all ten of my toes, painted red."

I've yet to summon the nerve to ask God to put a DSW Shoe Warehouse nearby, so I can buy cheap designer shoes for those feet.

But I will.

We get so bogged down, we forget how easy it is to pray. All you have to do is say hi. If we go through a tough time, we think we're bad people, that God couldn't love us. But He does. And that's all the preachin' I'm gonna do. You can always come back to God, no matter how long it's been.

> *Write yourself a permission slip to say hello to God, even if it's just in your head. He'll hear.*

part five

Permission to Get Better as I Get Older

When I was a teenager, forty was the age women lied about. You did not want to turn forty. In fact, if you looked decent, you could be thirty-nine until you turned fifty, at which point you'd say you were forty-three. The math was complicated but worth it, because forty was the end of youth, sex, and a flat stomach.

Forty is different now.

My generation is redefining how women lead the second half of their lives. How you feel about turning forty is a reflection of how you feel about your life. If you're dating a twenty-five-year-old, forty is the new thirty. If you're recovering from a C-section and a divorce, forty is just another obstacle.

A 40/40 among 20/20s

My spirits were low around my birthday because my marriage was cratering. I got a call from my girlfriend Ina.

"Sherri, put your halter top on, we're going out!"

I hadn't been out in forever. By *out*, I mean, dressed kinda sexy—showing skin, cleavage, and a ringless ring finger. I wore a nice wig and I put my eyelashes on. This was the old Sherri. *Still looking good*, I thought.

We went to Jay-Z's establishment, the ironically named 40/40 Club. A club I had no business being at, a club that was packed with hot, young 20/20s and sexy, sassy 30/30s. And one over-the-hill 40/40.

Everyone was dancing. Everyone but me.

"How you doin'?" I asked one guy.

"Good, how you doin'?" he said.

"Oh, good! I'm going through a divorce, my son is three, and he's a little bit of a problem right now but he'll be good once I bring the right man in."

He left.

"Girl," said another guy, "can I buy you a drink?"

"Well, I'm diabetic, so if you don't mind I'll keep sipping on this water. If my blood sugar gets too high, I could pass out."

He left. I walked back to my table.

"I just want to finish my appetizers and leave," I told Ina.

"Sherri," she said, "you got a glum look on your face. And you've got such a pretty smile. You've got to smile."

All right. I started grinning, hard. Baring my teeth at any man who walked by.

Nothing.

Maybe I wasn't smiling enough. I pulled my lips back as far as I could and jutted out my neck. I think my wisdom teeth were showing.

Nothing.

"Okay, Sherri," Ina said, "stop smiling. You look like an angry horse."

"What am I supposed to do?"

"Stand by the edge of the dance floor. Guys look tough, but they're shy. You're intimidating. Let them see that you're approachable."

That sounded reasonable. I tried not to feel sorry for myself. I looked at Ina. She wasn't looming over a dance floor to get some action. *That's okay,* I told myself, *you're just going to have to work harder, nothing new here.* I stood on the edge of the dance floor, holding my water. I started tapping my feet.

"Sherri, you're off the beat," shouted Ina, dancing with a hottie.

"That's because the only song I can hear is the one playing in my head, and it's called, 'Nobody Is Asking You to Da-aaaaance,'" I shouted back.

I watched Ina disappear into the crowd of young, happy dancers. Finally, a fish bit on my line.

"What do you do?" a young guy asked me.

"I'm a comedian. What do you do?"

"I'm in the studio," he said.

"In the studio?" I asked. Maybe I hadn't heard him right. These old ears.

"Yeah, in the studio," he said.

Nope, I'd heard right.

"What do you *do* in the studio?" For all I knew, he was killing people and burying their bodies there.

"Yeah," he said. That was his answer.

I tried again, but the more I pressed for specifics, the older I felt. I guess 20/20s don't care what a guy does, as long as he does it in the studio. I threw that fishy fish back in the water.

Another time, I was at a club, and I was just angry. Surrounded by youth and energy—I felt like punching something, but I was too tired to ball my fist. Why isn't a successful older woman like me as interesting as these broke young hotties? Isn't variety the spice of life? Damnit!

A guy walked up to me right as I was cursing the world.

"Excuse me, sister, excuse me," he said.

"No, young man, excuse *me*. You see all this right here?" I said, pointing to my entire body. "I paid for everything, my hair, my nails, my feet, I got it all, and I don't leech off no man to get it. Now what you want?"

"I was just going to tell you that you had some toilet paper hanging off your shoe."

I left.

> ***Write yourself a permission slip to dress up, go out, and leave your issues at home.***

Old enough to be your mother's friend

Younger men make me nervous. I couldn't date one; I'd live in fear that he'd catch me plucking a chin hair and run right into the arms of the nearest female not approaching perimenopause. One day, I was shopping at H&M. A young Puerto Rican guy was flirting with me from behind the counter.

"Go get with him," my girlfriend whispered.

"Oh, that sounds like a great idea," I said. My friend was in her thirties and kept trying to hook me up with pups. I needed to break it down for her. "I'll tell you what would happen if I 'got with' this little boy. We'd go to his family's house so he could introduce me to his mama. When he'd excuse himself to go to the bathroom, Mama will say, 'Excuse me, Sherri, but you and I went to high school together. What the hell do you want with my son?' And before I'd get to answer, she'll say, 'And what about children?'"

The thought of giving a grandchild to Denise from my graduating class made me so upset I left H&M without buying anything.

I was with my husband for a total of ten years. I missed out on a whole generation of come-on lines. Now I'm so rusty, I can't tell them apart from normal conversation. When I moved to a new apartment in New York, a Time Warner guy came to install a cable box. He looked out the window for a few seconds.

"You got a nice view out here. I like this view but . . . I love *this* view." Then he looked at me, up and down, left and right, north and south, east and west. You get my drift.

But I still didn't get it. Which "view" was he talking about? *The View* starring me, or the view *of* me? What if I flirt back and he's like, "Lady, back off. I meant *The View.* Jeez!" Then he's telling all his buddies back at the office that Sherri Shepherd hits on anything that walks into her apartment.

"If you have any problems," he said, giving me his card, "you be sure to give me a call."

Again, I was lost. Did that mean, "Let's have dinner" or did it mean, "Call me if the DVR doesn't get *Dancing with the Stars.*" Not that it matters. At this point in my life, *DWTS* is more important than dinner anyway. Maybe he'll read this book and let me know.

> *So write yourself a permission slip to be blunt. "If you're trying to get with me, blink twice."*

The intern learns a lesson

I'm still young enough to forget that I'm old. And it's humiliating to be reminded that you aren't young. There was an intern at *The View* who had just graduated from college, no older than twenty-three. She was standing next to me as I was saying good-bye to some audience members.

"Sherri, is this your daughter?" asked a lady from the front row.

I couldn't answer. I wanted to say, "Excuse me, I'm the mother of a three-year-old, not a twenty-three-year-old." But what really made me mad was the intern. She *should* have said, "Oh, Sherri's *way* too young to be my mother!" Instead, she giggled.

"No, she's not my mom, but she could be."

OH REALLY?

Ha ha. I laughed, but it was one of those laughs you give when you are pretending to be cool with something that you definitely are not cool with. The intern was too young to pick up on the subtleties of my fake laugh—that's why she was an intern. She was here learning basic life-work lessons like "Don't make fun of a senior staffer's age without getting said senior staffer to put, in writing, 'I am cool with that.'"

The intern started calling me "Mom."

"Hey, Mom!"

I let it continue for about two weeks. I tried to force myself not to mind. *Sherri, you're a comic, you can handle it.* One day, I admitted to myself that I was not handling it. I pulled the intern aside.

"Listen, if you want to keep your job, this Mom stuff has got to stop. You can call me 'Big Sis,' you can call me 'Auntie.' But do not—*do not*—call me Mom."

She stopped.

I agree that the intern had me on a technicality. I could have given birth when I was eighteen. And Lord knows, when I'm sixty, I'll probably be flattered if a twenty-three-year-old calls me Mom. But not yet, thank you.

It's depressing when young girls consider you a mother figure. I'm no longer competition. Young women don't clutch their men when I walk by. Instead they offer their assistance. I was standing on the bus recently and a young woman stood up.

"Excuse me, ma'am," she said. Ma'am? I was outraged. When did I go from miss to ma'am?

"Yes?" I said. *Be polite, Sherri,* I told myself, *she probably recognizes you from* The View.

"Would you like my seat?" she asked.

"No thank you!" I said. "I don't need your damn seat! I can stand up!"

And as soon as she got off the bus, I plunked down in her seat. My ankles hurt.

> **Write yourself a permission slip to explain to a young co-worker that you are not *freaking cool* like that.**

Mirrors, mirrors all over the walls

Age differences are painfully obvious when I shop for clothes. One day, I was at BCBG. I found a tight, formfitting dress, very short. Very Sherri. When I wiggled into it, I opened my eyes to preen in the looking glass, but instead wanted to cry. It had been a while since I'd been in a store with more than one mirror, and BCBG gave me at least eight different views of my behind. Mirror Number Five gave me the cruelest reflection—cellulite on my thighs and dimples on my knees. How did that happen? Why is there a package of hot dogs in my neck, and when did I get a hump? I was about to start sobbing when out walked a 20/20 wearing the *exact* same dress. She spun and twirled. The same mirrors that had just booed me like an Apollo crowd gave her a standing ovation. Mirror Number Five was trying to get her autograph.

She smiled at my lumps and rolls as if to say, "Grandma, stop it." I smiled back. "Bitch, if I was twenty years younger, you'd be putting on a burlap sack right now."

One of these things just didn't belong in that store, and it was me. Another dress I'd bought at BCBG I later saw on Lauren Conrad from *The Hills*. I thought, *What if* The Star *does a "Who Wore It Better?" How am I gonna beat Lauren Conrad?* I stopped wearing it. If she's shopping at BCBG, I need to bring my credit card to Chico's.

It's hard to know when you're supposed to pull out of the race. Madonna stayed in a lot longer than most women, but even she is starting to look gaunt. I look at Madonna the way that girl at BCBG looked at me: "Put that dress down. You're just going to hurt yourself."

Photoshop is the new Botox

I've seen a lot of these celebrities up close. If you ask me, their anti-aging secret is Photoshop, because they don't look half as good in person as they do in print. The geek who invents a "blur" tool that you can apply to your face in real life will be richer than Bill Gates. It's childish, but I like to think of celebrities leading normal, unglamorous lives. In fact, when I fantasize these days, it's not about sex or men. It's about celebrities who aren't able to escape the aging process. Maybe Goldie Hawn puts her teeth in a glass every night, and she wakes up early, before Kurt opens his eyes, to pop them back in. Maybe Charlize Theron keeps a Depends in her handbag. I don't know if it's true, but thinking it is sure feels good.

Technically, I'm a celebrity, but I don't feel like one. I don't go out much. When my son has a temper tantrum, I don't feel famous. When I mash oatmeal with bananas and watch it get thrown on the floor, I don't feel famous. And when I wipe a snotty nose with the hem of my own T-shirt, I feel downright anonymous. The only time I feel famous is when I show up to an event and people are expecting "Sherri Shepherd from *The View*." Otherwise, I'm a hermit. I stay at home, wigless, wearing a big T-shirt and sweatpants. Half the time I look like a just-released prisoner.

I was invited to a red-carpet event recently, saluting older stars. *Every* star had had massive amounts of work done. It was one sarcophagus after another. One famous lady (nameless—sorry, I'm not the *Enquirer*) almost made me scream. Her skin was pulled so tight, her face looked like a death mask.

Eventually, your face is going to reflect the life you led. I earned my stretch marks, and I got a great kid to show for them. These lines that I sometimes hate also prove that I've made it this far on my journey. I don't want to change the way I look, although I understand why other people do.

This business will drop-kick you the moment you have a crinkle near your eye. But you can't freeze-frame your face *and* move forward. It's one or the other. When I watch a movie and the actress can't even move her face—hey, it's called a *move-ee* for a reason. Move your dang forehead. You can't express every emotion your character feels through your lips. Your mouth ain't that talented.

When I was a kid, I used to drape a white towel over my head and pretend I had long blond hair. I wanted to be white. Now that I've seen the effects of the plastic surgery some older white women have had, I'm so grateful that my skin is black. Black skin is oily and saturated. I don't need Botox or Restylane—I barely even need moisturizer. All those young black girls out there feeling underappreciated? Just stay strong, you'll get yours in your second act.

Checking a different box

When you're young, ageism is not a problem you care about. I'd hear older actresses complain about it, but I felt like, *Hey, it doesn't affect me, and hopefully by the time it does, I'll be rich and famous and won't care.* Well, now that I'm forty, I do care. That older actress talking about ageism? That's me. It's painful to "age up." When you audition for a role, you check a box that is your "age range." It's the age you can get away with onscreen, not your actual age. Recently, I stopped checking "25–35." That hurt. I took a good, long look at myself and realized that I've moved up to the "masters" division.

When it comes to aging, stand-up comedy isn't as tough on women as the rest of show business. Of course, club owners will slather over a hot, young female comic, but when you've got a sold-out house, a young hottie ain't gonna wreck the room. Comedy is an art form where you *have* to be imperfect. That's what makes you funny. Young and pretty isn't as funny as old and pissed off about it. That's all the audience cares about. *Will you make me laugh? I paid a lot of money for these two drinks, and I need a laugh.*

> **Write yourself a permission slip to make the age you are right now the new forty.**

My son will be a great husband one day

I worry about being alone, but it's okay to just chill out. Being alone doesn't mean I'm gonna die alone. I would like to be in a relationship. I miss having discussions, sharing dreams, laughing at the neighbors, and being touched. I can't spend the rest of my life hoping the cable guy accidentally bumps into me. But for now, I'm focusing on being Jeffrey's mom. And I treat that poor three-year-old like he's my man, anyway. I'll come home from work, and he'll crawl into my lap.

"Mommy read," he says, handing me *Green Eggs and Ham*.

"Hold on. Let me tell you about my day."

"Mommy no. Mommy read."

"In a second. Do you know what so-and-so said to me in the dressing room?"

"Mommy mad."

"And that's before the Dow dropped a thousand points!"

"Mommy dow drops."

"EXACTLY! Jeffrey, it's so nice to have a man around the house who knows how to listen. Now let's read *Green Eggs*."

"And Ham!"

"No ham, baby. The Dow dropped, we can't afford ham anymore."

Where did I put my hustle?

Sometimes I feel bad that my son is getting a mom who has lost some of her hustle. Let's face it, I'm freaking tired. A lot. My knees hurt, I get this ache in my left butt cheek, and I'm cold all the time. I see young girls wearing tank tops in winter. Either they don't feel the cold, or looking sexy is so important that they don't care. But me? I can barely take Jeffrey outdoors if it gets below eighty degrees.

"What did you do this weekend?" someone at *The View* asked one Monday morning.

"Sat around the house."

"Did you take Jeffrey out?"

"Nope. We both sat around the house, watched TV, and we loved it."

"But there's so much to do in New York. There's a children's museum, there's a—"

"I know, and we're not doing it," I said. "I did hold him to the windowsill on Saturday afternoon, pointed to the park, and said, 'Look, Jeffrey, there's a boat.' Then I put him back on the couch and we watched SpongeBob and ate a few potato chips. It was a nice weekend."

Honestly, what's the point of having a view of the park if you can't substitute it for the real thing when you're tired? And I know I'm not alone. When I do make it outside to the real park, it's full of forty-year-old moms with twins. And we're all sprawled on the bench, exhausted. Not even opening our eyes if our kids fall and start crying.

"Be careful!" That's all us old moms say.

The young moms are running around, tending to cuts and giving hugs. If Jeffrey falls and he needs a Band-Aid, he'd better hope he brought his own. It's BYOB for that guy. The young moms sit on the swings with their kids. I tried to go down a slide with Jeffrey exactly once and got stuck. I climbed up the stairs of a jungle gym and it seemed like someone added four inches to each step.

I'm the opposite of a helicopter mom. I'm more of a downed helicopter mom. I had a wing problem, and I've been grounded until further notice. My fantasy is raising my son from an armchair.

Sometimes I'm so appalled at how tired I am, I force myself to act thirty. I try to "get back on that bicycle." Literally, I bought a bike to ride around Central Park. I got a helmet, pads, tight shorts. I would've pulled it off, too, if I hadn't been so wobbly. I kept almost falling. The park was full of walkers, and I kept yelling, "Excuse me!" Because I wasn't sure I could navigate around them.

Well, one pack of jerks was taking up the entire walkway, so I decided to bounce on down to the street, and then bounce back up, once I'd passed them.

Ain't it weird how things turn into slow motion when you're

about to fall? For about sixty seconds, I saw the asphalt coming toward my face. Then I was lying on the ground. The pack of jerks stepped over me. One said, "Nawh, that's what you get."

So there you go. If I'd been seventeen, writhing on the ground, guys would've been tripping over themselves to help me up. But now I'm forty, crying, "I'm hurt, hurt! Anybody gonna help me, does anybody see the blood?"

And all I get was, "Nawh, that's what you get."

> *Write yourself a permission slip to slow it down. Redefining forty doesn't mean you have to act thirty.*

The upside of being a grannymom

I guess the bonus to having 40/40 Sherri for a mom versus 20/20 Sherri is that Jeffrey will know more, because I do. In my twenties, I knew nothing about politics. Now it's all I talk about. One time Meghan McCain was on *The View*. She'd written a children's book called *My Dad, John McCain*. She gave me a copy. The book is for kids age five to ten, so I figured, *Okay, Jeffrey can pick it up in a few years, once his reading skills improve.* Well, wouldn't you know it, *My Dad, John McCain* is Jeffrey's favorite book. I don't get it. This book is way over his head. There are almost no color pictures, and none of the text rhymes. It's just John McCain doing "soldier" stuff. John McCain falling out of an airplane, John McCain swimming in a river, John McCain crash-landing. My son loves it.

"John McCain, John McCain," he says.

"Jeffrey, this is a house of Democrats," I remind him.

"John McCain, John McCain."

"Keating Five! Remember the Keating Five, baby!"

"Want to read John McCain!"

"Baby, because of Barack Obama, you can be president. Obama's really opening up the—"

"JOHNMCCAINJOHNMCCAIN!"

Someone needs to point me to a children's book about Obama, because I might be raising a little Republican here. And my old trick of skipping pages doesn't work because Jeffrey has the book memorized. If I jump ahead, he makes me start over. So not only do I have Elisabeth Hasselbeck talking about being Republican most mornings, but every night I have to read John McCain's life story to my son.

That's what being an old mom will get you—a child who disagrees with your political philosophy. That, and long boobs.

Boobs that can mop a floor

I am in mourning for my boobs. When I see the young moms at the park, I can't help but stare at their breasts. I see 20/20s with two or three kids and boobs that stick out, boobs that are parallel to the ground below, and I want to cry. Being an old mom means your boobs will not bounce back after childbirth. Angelina Jolie can have three babies and a rack you can hang an umbrella on because she did it *young.* (Anything under thirty-three is young.) Me—I had one baby that I only carried for five months but I did it old. My boobs touch the ground so much that I should probably put them in shoes.

The change in my bustline has been the most depressing physical ramification of passing forty. I've had a love–love relationship with my boobs since I was about six. I looked at the women in my family, and I knew that I, too, would be blessed with a large chest. I looked forward to it, and when they finally came, they did not disappoint.

Despite my weight ups and downs, my boobs stayed perky well into my thirties. When I got pregnant with Jeffrey, they peaked, no pun intended. I had 1950s porn star boobs. Full as pillows, pointing true north. I could have comforted an army of men with my pregnancy bosom. And within two months of Jeffrey's birth, my boobs had migrated south for a permanent winter. Now, some days, I can't even find them. They hide in my armpits, or they get tucked into my underwear.

I blame the breast pump.

Jeffrey was in the hospital for a long time, so I couldn't breastfeed. But I could pump. No one tells you about the breast pump, and I'm convinced if I'd ever seen one in action, I never would've gotten pregnant.

If you are considering motherhood, you should skip the next few paragraphs; you do not want to know about this.

The pump is actually two suction cups. They recommend that you pump one breast at a time—the pros can pump both boobs simultaneously. But let's not get too advanced right away. Where were we? Oh yes, there is a suction cup on your nipple. It's attached to a hose, and the hose is attached to a cup. That's where the milk goes. If this sounds like the same process that dairy cows go through, that's because it is.

You are a dairy cow.

It's important to position your nipple exactly in the center of the cup, or the machine will suction the areola, and that will hurt. And possibly cause blood vessels to burst, which makes your already unattractive boobs just a little grosser. So center that nipple, Mom.

The machine allows you to adjust the level of suction. For example, your first time, you would put the level on 1. And not much would happen. So maybe you would jack it up to 10.

"OH MY GOD!" you would scream.

Ten is too high. Try 5 and see what happens. After you find the right suction level, you should look away. Seriously, stop looking at your boob, because in about a minute, you will cry. Your beautiful nipple, that little nub your man likes to tickle and twist, is about to become disfigured. With each heave from the machine, your nipple gets stretched farther and farther until it is literally three inches long.

Now, you would expect that the sacrifice of your femininity would at least yield a cupful of milk.

Well, that depends. Some women are loaded with milk, while others pump and pump and come away with a few ounces.

Now, you might think, *Well, Sherri, that's okay, at least I can get some reading done, or catch up on TV.*

No you can't. You have to hold the suction cup with your hand. Now, there's a few sites on the Internet that show you how to hook the suction cup to your bra strap, with rubber bands, but you have to be MacGyver to do it right and sometimes the cups pop off. Did I mention that it hurts, too? And you can't watch TV unless you have your own TV in a private room, because you cannot be seen pumping breast milk. If your man sees you with cups on your boobs, your nipples out to your knees, and your pregnancy stomach sticking out, you won't have sex for months. Because you look like a mom now, not a woman.

My breasts today are like a museum piece. If you squint, you can imagine what they looked like before The Fall. Now they are housed with the rest of my body, in antiquities.

> *Write yourself a permission slip*
> *to take naked photos of yourself now,*
> *because no matter how "bad" you look,*
> *in twenty years, you're gonna look worse.*

My tummy, like the earth, is not flat

Actually, my boobs aren't the only body part that didn't bounce back. Like many older moms, I had a C-section. The cut is across your beautiful belly, and when it heals it's like having a slight Mona Lisa smile beneath your belly button nose. And the skin on top of the smile *hangs over* the skin beneath it. Like a shelf. If your boobs are long enough, they can rest on that C-shelf.

So, in addition to everything else, I have a wad of fat that pops out neatly over my underwear. This C-shelf is so pernicious, it actually pushes my jeans down below it. Sometimes, I think my C-shelf wants to stick out. *Why you hiding me, Sherri? Stop tucking me in a pair of Levi's, I want to see the world.*

If I have another baby, I'm getting a tummy tuck at the same time. In fact, I will have two teams of doctors on standby, plastics and obstetrics. As soon as my water breaks, I'll call plastics and tell them to meet obstetrics at the hospital. The moment I hear the baby cry, I'll kick obstetrics out of the room. "Make way, make way! Plastics in the house!"

I'm content to let my face age, but damn, I want my belly back. Back in the day, when my top popped up a bit, you'd see my cute little belly button. Now, when my top pops up, you see a

Mona Lisa smile and the C-shelf. The belly button? Gone. I can't find it. That slovenly lady that I used to make fun of, scratching herself on a street corner? That's me now.

My outfits don't help. Those high heels I used to wear at comedy clubs? And walk home in while I was cutting through MacArthur Park? No more. It's gym shoes now. White gym shoes. With black pants. The first thing I ask a shoe salesman is, "Does this have an arch inside?"

What part of no don't you understand?

Emotionally, getting older kicks ass. For one thing, I'm becoming indifferent to your opinion of me, and I like that. I used to be one of those people who said yes to everybody because I wanted to be liked. *No* was not part of my vocabulary. I was constantly stressed out. Now I freely tell people, "I can't do it." If someone asks for time or money, I say, "Yeah, I got it, but I'm not going to give it to you."

Without apology.

It's a wonderful thing to say no and not take on the guilt that's associated with it. Just keep moving forward. One thing that would drive me crazy is when people would stay at my house. And never leave. One girlfriend was having a tough time.

"Sherri," she asked, "you know, girl, can I come and stay with you for a minute 'cause I'm just trying to get myself together."

Every bone in my body was screaming *No,* except the bones in my mouth, which said, "Sure!"

We'd been great friends. I learned later that the key to our great friendship was that we weren't living together. My experience with "houseguests" is that when they don't give an end date, that's a bad sign. "Till Friday" can mean through Sunday. "Till next month" can mean two months. But "for a minute" is so unrealistic that it can mean anything, or in this case, six months.

She moved in. I noticed a pattern pretty quick. In the middle of the month, she'd say, "Oh, I can give you a little something," meaning money. At the end of the month, when rent was due, she'd say, "Oh, I ran out."

Meanwhile, she's having dinners at Cheesecake Factory and drinking bottled water at the movies—and not matinees. Full price, evenings. This arrangement lasted half a year because I didn't want to hurt her feelings.

After that, I started lying. If someone wanted to crash, I'd say, "No, I can't. I have a lot of stuff going on and I can't." And when they'd ask for specifics, I'd cook up an injured-relative story.

"My aunt broke her leg and my grandmother might be coming to stay."

"Sherri, I thought your grandmother passed on?"

Shoot. "That's right, she did, but my aunt still broke her leg."

Remembering lies was too much work. Something clicked when I turned forty. I worked up the courage to say, "No, you can't stay." Followed by silence. No explanation, because none is needed. You can't stay.

Lately, I've had a lot of requests for money. People think if you're on TV, you have "extra" money. Thank goodness I'd had some practice saying no by the time those requests began to accelerate. If I'd been twenty years old when I got *The View*, I'd be broke right now. When someone asks me for a loan these days, I'm old (and bitchy) enough to say, "Sorry, can't do it."

It's hard to explain how liberating that is. I come home, and nobody's in my house. Just me and Jeffrey. And I'm not mad at a friend because I loaned her money and she hasn't paid me back. My home is for my son and me, and we cherish our privacy.

> *So write yourself a permission slip to tell white lies that serve you. And keep notes, because you're old now and you will forget what you told that deadbeat friend of yours.*

Revenge of the nerd

A great way to appreciate your maturity is to attend your high school reunion. Don't worry about losing weight first; just show up and notice how your new, old self reacts to people who terrorized, humiliated, or ignored you. I was so excited for my twentieth. These were my Chicago friends (I only went to high school in L.A. for my senior year). Since seventh grade, we'd been nerds together. Since high school, we'd been disliked together—by a popular girl whom I will call "Tammy."

Tammy was a person who had the power to make me feel like crap. Unwanted, like an outsider. We all have a Tammy in our past, and this one (like many of them) was a cheerleader.

The usual reunion stuff was happening . . . Classmates recognize you, and you try to look at their name tags discreetly so they don't think you're a jerk. By the end of the night, I had sympathy with men who do boob checks. Boy, you gotta move them eyes fast to avoid getting caught.

My girlfriends and I regressed into giggling fifteen-year-olds. We were drinking, laughing, reminiscing . . . when who rolls up on us but Tammy.

Freakin' Tammy.

I had to glance at her name tag because she looked nothing like her young self. She had pockmarks on her face and smoker's skin.

"Hi, Sherri," she said. She was not smiling.

"Pick me!" I said. Wait, no. That's what I wanted to say. Because I really wanted to go back in time and get freakin' Tammy to sit next to me at lunch or pick me for her track team, so I wouldn't have been standing there, alone and unwanted on the floor of the gym.

"Hi, Tammy!" I said in real life. The reunion disappeared in the background, and it was just me and her. I was an outsider again. A black girl. The black girl.

"People tell me that you're on TV," she said, smoking, hard, like her cigarette was second-hand and the previous owner had sucked all the menthol out of it. "But I've never seen you before. I've never seen you on *anything*."

For a second, I felt like I hadn't been on anything worth seeing. All these years later, and she still got me. Then it occurred to me . . . why the heck is freakin' Tammy bringing up my career if she's not aware of it? I didn't mention I was on television, I was just dancing with my friends. I looked at her angry face and I realized that freakin' Tammy has seen *everything* I've ever done. She probably has my name on her TiVo list. And not just my name, but Cybill Shepherd's and Cheri Oteri's, too, just in case. Freakin' Tammy was freakin' lying to me.

"You haven't, huh?" I said. "Well, that's okay. Maybe next time." Yes, bitch, I will be on television again.

Freakin' Tammy walked away. That's when I realized I was

happy. Even though my marriage had ended and I was raising my son alone, I was doing okay. And I didn't need to list all the TV shows I'd been on. (Like she hasn't seen *Friends* or *Everybody Loves Raymond*, not even once. Girl, *please*.) I was comfortable enough in my own skin to let her think she beat me.

Even now, we'll go to commercial break on *The View* and I'll think, *Freakin' Tammy's watching right now*.

It was a relief to accept myself. To say, "I'm a mom. I'm a daughter. I'm a friend. I love being here. And I don't remember anybody's name. I want to dance! Even if I'm at the wrong reunion, let's dance."

I can't wait to go to my twenty-five-year reunion. I bet ten bucks that Tammy will say, "I heard you wrote a book. I haven't read it."

> **So write yourself a permission slip to forgive the Tammy in your life. Because after success, forgiveness is the sweetest revenge.**

The redefinition of a lot

Being mature means having perspective on your place in the world. Once, on *The View*, I joked about my diaries.

"Jeffrey's gonna read those things one day and go, 'My mama slept with a lot of men.'"

Whoopi Goldberg gave me that look: *Watch what you say, it's gonna come back to you.* I got worried and withdrew for a few minutes. Then I just let it go. A couple of years ago, I would've driven everyone on staff crazy. "Did you hear what I said? What am I gonna do! Oh my gosh! Can you bleep that?" And these nice people would've had to waste their time telling me that it didn't matter, that I was funny, blah blah blah.

Now I shrug those things off. I don't want to waste anyone's time. We all got kids to get home to. I say a dozen ridiculous things a week, and that one will simply be number 4,045. If my son does ask me about sleeping with a lot of men, I'll fudge a little.

"Define *a lot*, Jeffrey, because to your mom, that's three."

The joys of peaking during menopause

I'm very surprised I'm here. Reasonably successful and able to take care of my family. I chose a business that never allows you to feel safe. Just because you sign a four-year contract doesn't mean you have a job for the next four years, or even next week. I'm always convinced that every day is my last day on *The View*.

Politics had never been a passion of mine. Of course I studied current events in high school, but I wasn't personally invested, because Jehovah's Witnesses don't vote. And because I didn't vote, I didn't feel like I could complain. So I never even ragged on the government. The great thing about voting is I finally get to complain about taxes. I can't believe I missed out for all those years.

Regarding the federal government, the Witnesses follow the Bible scripture that goes, "We're in the world but we're not of the world." They interpret that to mean that everything is temporary, and the government will be replaced when Jesus returns. Witnesses pay taxes and abide by the law, but casting a vote is being "of the world." Frowned upon.

When I started on *The View*, I was replacing Star Jones, who was a lawyer and a legal analyst. She had a lot more education than I did, and she was comfortable expressing her opinions. I, on the other hand, was a mother, comedian, and actress, in that order. Oh, and my husband cheated on me. So that's what I was bringing to the table.

I had to catch up. Joy, Barbara, Whoopi, and Elisabeth were holding my hand, saying, "Whatever you need, we want to help you along on this journey." But I was starting from so far behind! I felt like one of those runners in a huge marathon. The ones who are so far back that by the time the winner has finished the race, they're just about to start.

I started reading everything.

Keeping up with the Behars

Factcheck.org, Wikipedia, *The New York Times, The Washington Post.* I felt like Sarah Palin did right after she was nominated, except I had to debate four Joe Bidens, every day. My routine quickly became (1) put the baby to bed, (2) pull out newspapers and magazines, and (3) read. When my eyeballs hurt, I'd watch cable TV and then transcribe what I heard onto my laptop because that extra step helps me remember things correctly.

It's fun.

Well, not fun "at a club" fun, but that's not fun anymore, either. I believe that knowing the issues is important for my son. So I can help create a better world for him, so he can create a better world for himself. And so on. I want to create a new dynasty of well-informed, voting Shepherds. Because I no longer think Armageddon is gonna get me, but I'm afraid that global warming will. I committed the terms of the first bailout to memory because I'm a mother.

Now, on *The View* I sit between a hard-core Republican and a hard-core Democrat, and that's probably where I sit philosophically, too. I probably lean more toward Joy and Whoopi, now that I'm analyzing the issues. That might surprise people who think all evangelicals are conservative.

Sometimes I surprise myself. I have been taken far, far out of my comfort zone on *The View*. And because I'm *just* old enough to not care if you like me, I will stand up in an argument where I once would have stood down. But I don't care for debates. I learned to role-play when I was a Witness, but I never liked it. I was always uncomfortable grilling people about their faith, trying to corner them with scripture.

I've been in confrontations with Elisabeth that have left my back in spasms. I don't like exploding or losing control. I'm used to being funny. I like to get a laugh. Feeling a catch in my throat because I think I'm gonna cry or shout or hurl is stressful.

And yet sitting a few feet away from Barbara Walters is something beyond my wildest dreams. I can't even say it was a dream, because what single mom/comedian in her right mind would think she'd be working with Barbara Walters? She is an icon, and is personally responsible for a serious fissure in the glass ceiling. It's like getting a pilot's license and sharing a cockpit with John Glenn. I'm still astonished.

Can't I just do the food segments?

Usually, I do the comedic segments on *The View*. That's my comfort zone, being loud and goofy and silly. I will literally put egg on my face to get a laugh. One day, Barbara was scheduled to interview an American soldier and his Iraqi wife. Both of them had had their lives threatened. Their story was one of bravery and sadness.

"Sherri," she said, "I took Whoopi out of that segment. I want you to do it with me."

Whoa. This was definitely out of my comfort zone. I tried to joke my way out of it.

"Barbara, I just want to do the food segments so I can eat ribs."

Whoopi spoke up. "No, Sherri. You need to learn how to do the other things. You do the funny very well. Now you need to learn how to do the serious stuff."

"Oh, come on," I said, "I'm not trying to be Oprah!" What if I said something insensitive, or stupid? This couple had already been through enough.

My pleas fell on deaf ears. Hours later, I was sitting on the sofa, helping out the woman who'd once interviewed Fidel Castro. As far as I know, I didn't make a cultural gaffe. I've participated in quite a few serious interviews since then, and I always tell myself beforehand, *Channel Barbara Walters. Be serious and if you can, get a tear out of somebody.*

Most of the time, I'm the one that's crying.

I thought stand-up was the hardest thing I would ever do. I'm not one of those comedians who can wing it—just stand onstage, unprepared, and "be funny." I'd watch the comedians who work that way, weaving words in and out, getting the crowd into a fever pitch, and feel inadequate. I was a Salieri among Mozarts. I didn't fly by the seat of my pants, I wrote down my jokes. I made a set list. I came up with heckler lines in advance. I hustled to work, auditions, and clubs—most of the time on public transportation. None of it came to me easy.

Does Barbara know she hasn't fired me yet?

Yet my greatest professional challenge has been working on *The View*. Every day I come home and check for the voice mail that says, "Sherri, we're gonna go in another direction." Barbara picked up on these feelings and took me out to lunch.

"Sherri," she said, "if we didn't think that you could do this job, *believe me,* you would not be at that table."

Whatever my misgivings were about my own skills, Barbara Walters does not have time for unnecessary lunches. Giving me a pep talk probably meant she had to cancel an interview with Vladimir Putin.

"Speak up," she said. "You represent a lot of regular women."

That was a lightbulb moment for me. I thought, *Okay, Barbara has faith in me, and if she has faith in me, then what I have to say must be important.* I started being honest at the table. When Joy or Whoopi went off on something political, I'd interrupt them.

"I don't know what you're talking about."

That was hard to say, hard to admit. What did Lincoln say? "Better to remain silent and be thought a fool than to speak out and remove all doubt."

But as soon as I fessed up to getting lost in a conversation, I started getting e-mails and calls from women: "I didn't know what they were talking about, either. I was just as confused as you. Thank you."

> *So write yourself a permission slip to be honest about what you don't know. If my inbox is any indication, you're in good company.*

The only thing I will be remembered for

Of course, not all feedback is positive. In fact, something I said on one of my first official shows triggered a negative blowback that still hurts. Whoopi asked me if the world was round or flat and I responded with the blurt heard 'round the world.

"Is the world flat? I never thought about it."

Let's backtrack. Put yourself in my gym shoes. This is my second or third day on the show. I'm terrified. Nobody knows me very well, but they know I'm an evangelical Christian. Evolution was one of the Hot Topics. Some of the ladies at the table believe in evolution. I do not. I believe in creation. But as you know, I don't like to get in faith debates. Live and let live.

The ladies at the table, of course, love to debate faith. And they're good at it—they've had years of practice. And at this point, I've had two days. So when Hot Topics turned to evolution, I took it down a notch. *Please, Lord, not yet, I haven't even got my first paycheck yet.* Joy, Whoopi, Barbara, and Elisabeth batted the topic about. I kept praying.

God, I really would appreciate it if, somehow, someone were to bring up Project Runway. *'Cause I watched it last night, and I am all over it.*

"Is the world flat?" Whoopi asked. She was looking at me.

"Is the world flat?" I repeated, buying time.

"Yes," said Whoopi.

Shoot, she wants an answer. God, I know You're busy, but if there's any sort of Paris Hilton segue that You can help me think of right now, that would be great.

"I don't know," I said.

Whoopi's mouth was moving again, but I didn't hear words come out. Instead, it was some kind of gibberish, followed by a peaceful white noise. I think my reaction must have been a reflex, a kind of instinctive "intense-debate" reflex action, because I was transported to another part of my head. It was quiet there. Financial worries floated by, like little clouds. *How the heck did that check bounce? Am I gonna get a bill collector calling me? Can I get cash from my ATM?*

"Brzzzzzzz," said Barbara.

"Fdssssssssfd," said Whoopi.

Why aren't they speaking English? And why are they talking so slow? Are we still taping? Everyone was staring at me, waiting for me to say something.

"I don't know," I said, hoping for a fill-in reply. Maybe Elisabeth would say, "Sherri, what do you mean you *don't know* what happened on *Project Runway*?" So I could jump in and save myself.

"Huusrfrrrrr," said Barbara, "your son!"

Jeffrey? How did we start talking about Jeffrey?

"All I know is that I got to raise this son," I said. *All right—who in their right mind is gonna debate that?*

"Drsssssssssxx," said Barbara, "what if your son asks you wfffdddsalk."

"I don't know," I said. *How come we haven't gone to commercial yet?* "We'll go to the library."

I don't remember much after that. Hot Topics ended, the show ended. Barbara leaned over to me.

"Dear," she said. Her voice was back to normal. Everyone's was, actually. *Thank God, I'm not going crazy.*

"Yeah?"

"The earth is round."

"I know, Barbara."

"Well, you just said on the show that you didn't know if the earth was round or flat."

"I said what?"

"You said that you didn't know if the earth was round or flat," she said, gently, "so I'm telling you that it's round."

"Oh my goodness."

Since I didn't remember most of the conversation, I didn't realize how badly I'd embarrassed myself. In hindsight, I probably shouldn't have gone on the computer that day. Or that year, actually.

My Web site had crashed.

"You're as dumb as a 3rd grader," read one e-mail. Or was it every e-mail? I was the second most Googled person in the country that day. I was written about in the newspaper, "New *View* host doesn't know if the earth is round." People said Barbara made a mistake hiring me. One of my favorite TV shows, *Best Week Ever*, called me an idiot. Joel McHale of *The Soup* called my comments "the stupidest thing I've ever heard."

I was crushed. I made a mistake at work, and instead of one secretary seeing it, twelve million people saw it. And a couple of them put it on YouTube, so twelve million more people saw it after their co-workers said, "Dude, Google Sherri Shepherd and earth." You can still see it. So can your children and your children's children. When Jeffrey gets older, and I yell at him because he forgot to bring home some milk, he can go to the computer, pull up that YouTube clip, and say, "At least I didn't forget the earth was *round*."

The very next show, I explained that I'd had a brain fart. I think people believed me, but try Googling that video. No one forwards the correction clip to their friends. I finally realized that I live in a time when a silly two-minute conversation will follow me to my grave, and there's nothing I can do about it. However, since I have your attention, let me state, for the record, that I *know* that the earth is round.

But I still don't believe in evolution.

> *So write yourself a permission slip to say the dumbest thing in the world. 'Cause, thanks to me, no matter what you say, it will be the second dumbest thing in the world.*

Jokes that should be heard, not read

Another time, I gave an interview to *Precious Times,* which is a magazine aimed at black Christian women. That's when I got to learn two more lessons. One: Jokes come across different in print than when they're coming out of your mouth. Two: Quotes without context can make you look horrible. In this interview, I talked about feeling inadequate when it came to discussing my faith at the table. I lacked eloquence and I was having trouble sticking up for myself. My joke was that if Juanita Bynum was at that table, she could lay hands on Barbara and save her. I intended that joke to be about me—how klutzy I felt—not Barbara (or Juanita). But on paper, it came across like I thought Barbara Walters was a heathen.

I had to apologize for that. Barbara totally understood.

I also discussed a low point, before I was saved, when I'd had many abortions. I wanted women who are ashamed of their abortions to know that Jesus forgives them. That's what I was trying to say. Well, the only sentence that made it to print was, "I've had more abortions than I can count." It made me sound cavalier and flippant, like I was bragging.

Cue apology number two, or ten. Heck, I should just draft a Mad Libs apology that I can alter every week.

I apologize for saying ____. What I meant by that was ____. If I offended ____, ____, or ____, I am ____. Now let's talk about ____ Spears, Corey ____, or *Dancing with the Stars*.

It's learn-as-you-go on *The View*. At least I'm old enough to handle it. No matter what I do the rest of my life, some people are only going to think of me as that lady who's "as dumb as a 3rd grader."

Not trying to convert anyone

That's okay. I say a lot of things people disagree with. But Barbara asked me to be part of the show because she wants my point of view. Now, when I start talking, my attitude is, *"Here's what I have to offer and if you don't like it, Whoopi or Joy or Elisabeth has probably got something you will like. But somebody likes what I'm putting out. And if you don't, move out of the way of the person that does. Down in front.*

And since I'm clearing the air, please understand that when I talk about my faith at the table, I'm not trying to convert anybody to Christianity. I was bad at field service as a kid, and I'm bad at it today. When the subject comes up on *The View*, I am happy to share what Jesus did for me. If you and I meet in person and you press me, I'll tell you what Jesus can do for *you*. And that's as far as I'll go. If you don't agree, I still love you. Hopefully you still love me. Now let's go get something to eat. (Not Pinkberry.)

I'm lucky to work with women who can also leave it at the table. After the camera turns off, we're still friends. No one says, "Oh, you're stupid. Your opinion doesn't matter. How could you?! Where did you get that from?"

We talk about Iraq and Obama and we're shouting and interrupting. Then we come back from commercial and it's "Up next, how to dress a turkey."

People think there's no way we could be friendly after a heated conversation. But it happens because we have a genuine respect for one another. I'm not trying to change your opinion and you're not trying to change mine. We're just trying to bring some stuff to the table.

And then . . . a worse gaffe machine than me!

Witnessing Sarah Palin's rise and fall was very interesting to me. Like a lot of women, I was really inspired by her story. Mother of five, one with Down syndrome, a female in a male-dominated profession. After Hillary conceded, I needed to see that. Hillary's loss in the primary was devastating to me. And seeing Sarah getting hazed after coming to national prominence from out of nowhere, well, I had empathy for her. When people started laughing at her lack of experience, I got mad. It felt like they were disrespecting the experience that comes from raising five children. It sounded sexist. Like they were laughing at me, at the women who watch our show.

Finally, I decided that Sarah Palin wasn't the right woman to be vice president. Once I got a good look at her temperament and her positions on issues, I didn't care that her life was inspiring. I could not vote for her.

Sarah Palin reminded me of a great-looking pair of shoes. You see them at the store, and you try them on, they're not completely comfortable, but damn they make your legs look good. You make an impulse buy. Then you get home and start breaking them in on the carpet. And you realize these shoes are not right. The heels are too high, the tip is squishing your toes. After a few hours, your back hurts and you've switched back to your gym shoes. You end up returning them. Sarah Palin, too, seemed like a great idea, until I took her home and tried her on. She was too tight and I returned to the other ticket.

Politics aside, I have *one* toddler and I can barely keep my eyes open to do an hour of work every day. Sarah Palin is a few years older than me, has five kids, and one is an infant with special needs. If she were to get a call at 3 AM, who's to say she's not gonna instinctively hit the snooze button? That's what I would do. At first, it was fun for women to think, *Well, it's about time that someone like me is in the White House.*

Then you start looking at how you run your life, and how you barely know where North Korea is on a map, and you realize, *America deserves better.* Hillary should have been our president because she isn't like us. She is *way* smarter. I believe Hillary Clinton wasn't fully appreciated until Sarah Palin came along. Now we can look back and say, "That's what a female candidate for president should look like and sound like."

I'm tellin' ya, these broads rawk

This decade, the "aughts," is a great time to hit your forties. And I'm luckier than most actresses. Instead of working with young starlets who obsess about their wrinkles, I'm knocking heads with real women who obsess about issues.

Joy Behar didn't even start doing stand-up until she was forty. She was divorced, she needed money to take care of her daughter. That's where I am now! Whoopi is re-peaking. She's earned every award possible in show business and she's still growing, still pushing herself. Elisabeth is in her thirties and she's the baby. And Barbara Walters? She doesn't sleep. Her schedule would exhaust a vampire. If she'd never created *The View*, she'd still be the most respected newswoman in the business. But her greatest success occurred after age thirty-five. These are my mentors. I feel like I'm just getting started.

When I walk down the hallway and see my photo on the wall with the other ladies, I still pinch myself and yelp a little.

"Hot damn! I'm on *The View*!"

It's easy for us older women to feel like we're finished. Like we don't matter anymore, and it's not true. Our bodies are changing, but our minds are just starting. We all have a second act, and a third.

> *So write yourself a permission slip to step outside your comfort zone. Because it may end up being the beginning of your new one.*

part six

*Permission to Be
Less Than Perfect*

Diabetes sucks.

You're probably saying, "But Sherri, you *just* said that you thank God for diabetes, because it saved your life."

Oh, I know. And I do thank Him, but that doesn't change the fact that diabetes sucks. I don't blame God, I blame me. That's how far gone I was. The only thing that got me to stop numbing myself with food was the fear of losing my foot. And even then, my first thought was, *Shoot, how am I gonna walk to the refrigerator without feet?*

I am a hardheaded woman, I always think I know what's best. Sometimes I forget that God always points me down the right path. Before I was diagnosed, He would often gently suggest that I ease up on the cake.

"Sherri, there's about ten reasons that ain't good for you."

"Thank You for Your concern, God, You're sweet," I'd say, licking frosting off my fingers. "But You have apparently mistaken me for a diabetic. Now, I understand that You're busy with hurricanes, tornadoes, and shoplifters, and every once in a while, mistakes happen. I promise not to tell anyone. So if You'll excuse me, I gotta finish off these cookies before they go stale."

Then I'd crunch just loud enough to drown out God's reply.

Yes, I have a listening problem. Maybe it's a hearing problem. If I believe what you're saying doesn't apply to me, I can't hear you. And after decades of whispering, nudging, and nagging, God finally had to yell. When I look back at my life, it's obvious that He tried other methods first.

Soaring diabetes rates in the African American community, of which I am a proud member?

Oh, that's them, not me.

My own family tree is knotted with diabetics?

Oh, that was them, not me.

I get diagnosed with *pre*-diabetes, which, untreated, always leads to full-blown diabetes?

Oh, that's other pre-diabetics, not me. Look, I'm Sherri. Bad things don't happen to me, okay? I'm protected. I got sprinkled with fairy dust when I was born. I got an angel on my shoulder. I got—

"Diabetes," said my doctor, shaking her head. "We're going to put you on medication. And here's a needle. You'll be checking your blood three times a day for the rest of your life."

Excuse me?

Raised by a tribe of peglegs

As an adult, I have been shocked to find that many people in the United States do not have a dining table large enough to accommodate a relative in a wheelchair. I genuinely believed that what united us as Americans was our one-legged uncles. Amputation and blindness were unremarkable in my family. For instance, while I knew that babies were supposed to be born with ten toes, it was news to me that they're supposed to keep them beyond the age of fifty. During my wedding vows, I think I promised to love my husband, "in sickness and in health, with one foot or two."

I always thought they should have made a sequel to *My Left Foot*, and called it *You're Taking That, Too?* I thought amputation was part of the aging process. That's probably why I bought so many pairs of shoes in my twenties—I wanted to wear 'em while I had a place to put 'em.

Now here is another shocker. Despite the fact that diabetes is all over my family like whipped cream on a pumpkin pie, I was never made aware of it, or even told how to avoid it. Every once in a while, I'd hear vague notions about various family members.

"Did you hear about your uncle? He got *the sugar.*"

"The sugar," of course, was diabetes. That's how common diabetes was in my family—we gave it a cute nickname, like it was the family dog. My grandfather and grandmother had the sugar, and my aunt, sister, and cousins live with the sugar.

Now I know that fatal, hereditary diseases should not have adorable nicknames. Women whose families have a history of breast cancer do not call it *"the cancie."* I can Monday-morning-quarterback my family's history and see that our tragic error was in not taking diabetes seriously. Not even after we were diagnosed with it. My aunt refused to change her diet, even after she went blind.

The American Diabetes Association indicates that almost 8 percent of our population has diabetes, and a quarter of them don't even know it.

> *Write yourself a permission slip to start wondering if you and yours are vulnerable.*

Where does your mom keep the needles?

When I was a kid, we had hypodermic needles all around the house. I remember being at a friend's house when I was a girl, wondering when her mom was going to shoot up some insulin.

Turns out that was another thing that isn't an "all y'all" experience!

My mom's diabetes was bad, and unfortunately she didn't do much to abate it. Yes, she'd give herself shots and check her levels with insulin strips, but I always saw her drinking fruit punch and eating cookies.

Doctors call diabetes "the silent killer," which sounds a heck of a lot more serious than "the sugar." It does internal damage first. If you're not looking for signs, you won't see them. Your feet might get a little numb, but that could be anything, right? *The cold, the heat, these dang shoes.* Then it goes away. Then your fingers start tingling, but that could be anything, right? *The cold, the heat, this dang computer.* Then it goes away. Then your vision gets blurry, but that could be anything. *You're getting old, you're tired, hey—your grandma wore glasses, right?* Then it goes away.

Until it stops going away.

I understand why people kid themselves into believing that they aren't as sick as they are. After a doctor gives you the information, the onus is on you to take care of yourself. Some people just can't do it.

My mom was rushed to the hospital many times for having low blood sugar. And every time, she came home and downed a huge pitcher of fruit punch.

Bottom line: We diabetics need to keep our blood sugar level consistent. When it gets too high or too low, our life is threatened, it's that simple. And that difficult. I didn't realize how bad my mom's health was until she started having "complications." Lots of seemingly unrelated illnesses are actually complications of diabetes, like stroke, kidney disease, hypoglycemia, and high blood pressure. In my mom's case, they seemed to come at once, like an avalanche. She lost the feeling in her feet, and her vision got worse. Her trips to the hospital became more frequent.

The last time she checked into the hospital, the doctor told us her prognosis looked grim. She had fallen into a coma.

"We need to amputate your mom's toe," he said.

"Well, okay. It's just a toe," I said.

"Well, no. That's the beginning. Her other toe is going to follow shortly thereafter. And then we're going to amputate the next one and then it's going to be her whole foot. The amputations won't stop," he said.

And while we grew up joking about diabetes, it wasn't a joke now. This thing was happening to my mom, and it was nothing short of horrible.

The hospital had put her on a life-support system. Our choice was to let her stay, unconscious, on a breathing machine, while doctors began taking off pieces of her body—or to let her go. We knew she would not want to live like that. So my sisters and I made the wrenching decision to take our mother off life support.

She was forty-one when she passed on. The sugar, and its complications, can take a person that fast.

What, me worry?

I was twenty-three when I lost my mom.

You're probably saying, "Wow, Sherri, I bet you took a good long look at yourself in the mirror and changed your eating habits right then and there."

Um, did you skip the other chapters, or are you being sarcastic? Because I did not give diabetes another serious thought until I was in my *late thirties*.

Listen, when I put on a pair of blinders, I secure them with superglue.

I saw a nutritionist when I was thirty-seven or thirty-eight. I was hoping to learn about a diet plan that would kick-start my metabolism and help me lose weight. He took some tests and sat me down, all serious-like: "Sherri, you are pre-diabetic."

"I'm diabetic?"

"No, you are pre-diabetic. You are borderline."

"So, I'm not diabetic."

"Not yet."

"So, technically, I can still eat pasta and cheesecake and stuff."

He got frustrated.

"I don't know how to make this more plain to you. This is urgent. Your glucose level and your A1c level—the level where your blood is—are so high, you might as well say you're diabetic."

"But I'm not diabetic?"

"No, you're not."

"Well, that's all I need to know."

And I didn't change a thing. Not one thing. I can't blame God—He tried.

I began to notice little things over the next year. My feet started to tingle, my toes would get numb. It bothered me enough to start praying.

God, I can't feel my left toe. If You bless me so that I don't have to get my feet cut off, I swear I won't eat another M&M.

The feeling would come back in my toe. And not an hour later, I'd be finishing the M&M's. My sister had just been diagnosed with diabetes, but still, I thought I was exempt. The blurry vision, the tingling—*it's got to be a coincidence.* If I could spend months cutting through MacArthur Park at 2 AM without getting attacked, no way was diabetes gonna get me.

Right?

If I'd gone to the doctor, I could've gotten an early diagnosis and saved my body some internal damage. But I was afraid. As long as nobody in a white coat told me I was diabetic, then I wasn't.

Right?

And as long as my vision kept clearing up, and the tingling subsided, I was okay to eat pasta until I passed out.

Right?

One of the signs of diabetes is extreme thirst. You keep running to the bathroom to pee. You constantly feel like you're about to wet yourself. And you run to the potty, certain you're moments from soiling your pants, but when you sit on the toilet, nothing. They say that amputees have phantom pain in their missing limb. Well, diabetics must have phantom pressure on their bladders. Back and forth, back and forth to the bathroom. That's when I got scared. My youngest sister, Lori, had been diagnosed a few years back, and that was how it started with her.

I knew. I made an appointment with a doctor. The first thing she did was measure my glucose.

"Okay, Sherri, it's really high. Let's do a test."

Ah, the four-hour glucose test. It's a classic. You eat a normal meal, then you don't eat anything for four hours. Then you get tested. Pretty simple, yet I was worried about those four hours without food. What if there was an earthquake during the third hour? What if I was stuck for ten days under rubble, waiting for a rescue dog to smell me, but he couldn't 'cause I'd wasted away? A lot can happen in four hours. For safety's sake, I decided to eat enough to carry me through an earthquake. I headed for the bomb shelter of restaurants, a pancake house.

"I'll have a full stack," I told the waitress.

"Okay, anything else?"

"Bacon."

"Okay, anything else?"

"Douse it all with strawberry syrup."

"Okay. Anything else?"

"I'll get back to you."

I must've sensed this was my last guilt-free binge, because I ate and ate and ate. I put syrup on *everything*, probably even in my coffee. I should've just stuck a straw in the bottle and finished it off. I walked to the doctor's office, prepared for a natural disaster. I stuck my arm out.

"Test me," I said.

When the doctor came back with my results, she was frowning.

"Damnit," she said.

I don't care who you are, you don't want your doctor to glance at your test results and swear.

"Good news?" I asked. I knew it wasn't good news. I tried to savor this last second of a normal life. Because once I knew I had diabetes, I would have to change everything.

"Sherri, oh boy. You're at 294," she said.

"What's normal?"

"One hundred."

I tried to save myself.

"It's from all that syrup. Let's do another one tomorrow."

"No. Sherri, you're going on medication. Immediately."

> *If any of this sounds remotely familiar to you, then write yourself a permission slip for that last binge. And then make an appointment with your doctor.*

Me and meds don't mix

You're probably saying, "So, Sherri, it sounds like you got scared straight and finally got your sh*t together—"

Stop right there. I didn't even fill the prescriptions. I hate pills. My sister had already started taking three kinds of medications, several times a day. She tells me she hasn't felt completely like herself ever since. Taking pills, every couple of hours, every day, rain or shine, is difficult. My mom would forget to take her pills, and then try to catch up.

Of course, I *considered* taking the meds, for about five seconds. Then when my doctor said, as she was ripping page after page of prescriptions off her pad, "Look, you're gonna get bloated. *In fact*, you're probably going to gain weight."

No thank you. I tore up the prescriptions and called my sister. She chewed me out.

"Sherri, your cholesterol is off the charts and so is your blood pressure. You could have a stroke."

"Lori, I'm not going to have a stroke until I'm, like, sixty."

"No, your cholesterol is so high that you could have a stroke today. And you think you're going to have any kind of sitcom with your face hanging off?"

One thing about family, they know where to twist the knife. Lori knew the deterioration of my health would not bother me, but my career? Hold on.

"That's not the kind of laughter you want," she continued, "people laughing at you because half your face is hanging like a painting. And you probably won't be able to use half your body. And where you gonna go with no foot? How many scripts do you read that call for women with no feet?"

Later that day, I was sitting on the stairs. I had just eaten pasta pesto—my favorite. I make it from scratch. I could feel the pasta sinking its teeth in my blood, draining me of whatever energy I had left. I prayed.

God, I'm supposed to start The View, *but I have no energy. My mind is foggy. What am I gonna do?*

I had a vision—a real vision, like the kind you read about in the Bible. The colors were vivid and surreal, an old Technicolor movie. Jeffrey was five years old, curled up on his bed, clutching his teddy bear. He was crying. All the moms had come to school that day, except his. He was asking where Heaven was, because that's where his mommy lived.

I felt like Scrooge, being visited by the Ghost of Jeffrey Future. I started crying. I didn't want my son to wonder where his mommy went, or have to decide whether or not to pull me off life support. I didn't want him growing up with a sick mom.

Finally, I could hear what God was telling me.

"Sherri, this could be your story. But it doesn't have to be this way."

That was my scared-straight moment. There should be a program like that for diabetics, *Scared Healthy*—where those who have been diagnosed with diabetes meet with someone who lost her mom as a kid. Just sit there and let her tell you what it was like. And then you imagine your kid feeling that way, for even a second. I dare any mom to ignore doctor's orders after that.

That day, I stopped eating pasta, soda, fruit punch, french fries—basically, everything delicious. I started eating healthy. Really healthy. I went from 187 pounds to 147 pounds, just as I was starting on *The View*. I began as a size 16 and went down to a size 4, all on television. I was on a mission to raise my son to adulthood.

People would stop me on the street.

"Sherri, girl, you doin' Weight Watchers?"

"Nah, I'm doin' diabetes."

People want to hear the fast solution. The fat blocker, some pill. What worked for me was, well, *work*. I started vegetables. Salmon, salad, and baked chicken. My rule was: *If it's boring, I'll have a bite.*

The doctor told me that my insulin levels had improved so much, I didn't need the medications.

> *Imagine all the lowlifes your daughter or son will be palling around with if you aren't there to stop it. Now, write yourself a permission slip to consider yourself important enough to stick around.*

Lose forty pounds in eighty days, with diabetes!

As a chubb for most of my life, the few times I've been thin have been wonderful. I wish I could tell you that being thin is as hard as being big, but it's not. You can walk into a normal store, rifle through the clearance rack, and find something that fits. Of course, I don't recommend getting diabetes, but the fear of death *did* help me get down to a size 6.

It was such a relief to wear clothes without flowers printed all over them. Have you noticed that anything above a size 14 is covered in chrysanthemums or geraniums? Being a 16 is already tough, now I gotta have a bouquet printed across my behind? Put me in some dang turquoise!

The lack of empathy for big women does not stop when you're famous. We've all seen celebrities walk the red carpet. Entertainment reporters ask who designed the dress. Well, I'm going to estimate that a full 100 percent of all designers do not want a big girl saying their name. Which is dumb, because most American women are over a size 14. But people do dumb things, and designers are no different. They don't want to be seen with us, they're ashamed we wear their clothes. (I say *us* because I always feel like a big girl, even when I'm thin.)

If you're a thin celebrity, photographers will take a thousand pictures of you. When you're a fat celebrity, they take one picture of you and that's only because you're standing next to a thin celebrity. Then they will crop you out of it. The next time you see a photo of a skinny celebrity, and right next to her you see a random petal, I guarantee you she was standing next to a big girl.

When a celeb appears at an event, her outfit is often put together by a costume designer. Since big girls are the least prestigious women to dress, they save us for last. And we can tell. The clothes they bring for us always look like they were bought that morning at the only Lane Bryant that was open. They'll grab a size 22, even if you're a 14, and pull it back with bobby pins. In show business, if you ain't a 0, you might as well be a 22.

For about five minutes, I was able to wiggle into a 4. *The View* was in Vegas, and the gloves came off, so to speak. I emerged from the Caesars Palace Hotel pool area in a bikini and paraded through the entire casino. It wasn't a string bikini, and I still had a few things covered up because I have had a child, but for the first time since my divorce, I felt *fine*. Like I could turn a head or two. Of course, my feet were tingling and I had to hire someone to massage my hands after they got numb. God is always reminding me, "Sherri—don't get cocky. You got something that can take you down."

Since I always think of myself as plump, I'm easy to impress when I'm thin. One time when I caught a replay of *The View*, I thought something was sticking out of my neck, like a lump. *Oh, Lord, I have cancer, too?* Then I realized that thing was my collarbone. I didn't think I even *had* one of those elegant knots. Collarbones seemed like things that soap actors had, not Shepherds. Yet there I was, looking all Susan Lucci at the table.

Also, my legs were crossed. Not at the ankle, not at the knee, but thigh over thigh. And it wasn't like the old days, where I had to lift my thigh, pull the fat back, and shove it on top of the other thigh. This time, I just lifted and crossed, like I was Elisabeth or something.

My weight vacillates. I go from small to medium to medium-large. I guess that's to be expected from someone who's writing an entire book on being imperfect. But I'm still striving to do better, to stay one size consistently.

I wish more diabetics could have visions like mine. A lot of folks think, *Well, it's just me.* They try to change their diet and they can't do it. They think they brought "the sugar" on themselves. I know darn well that if they were diagnosed with tuberculosis, they'd do everything they could to make themselves better—no one feels responsible for tuberculosis. But diabetes feels like your own dang fault for eating too much. And when you're in that place, it's hard to summon the self-esteem to start caring about yourself.

You must.

Your son does not want to change your underpants

When we don't take care of ourselves, we're being selfish, not self-less. As we descend into helplessness, our families step up to the plate. Every time I want to binge, I imagine Jeffrey, but he's not five, he's eighteen. Everyone's asking him where he's going to college and he's saying, "I'm not. I need to be home to take care of my mom. I have to change the wrappers on her foot, change her diaper. I'm just gonna sell stuff on eBay."

One of my cousin's friends quit his law firm job so he could move back home and take care of his uncle. Another friend had to move back to Mississippi to help take care of her cousin, who was thirty-five when she died. Before she passed, she lost her leg and her fingers. Imagine your children having to forgo their dreams to move back home and watch you deteriorate like that. My sister Lori spent so much time taking care of Mom that she barely graduated from high school. Nobody wants that for their children.

I lost my mom nineteen years ago and it still hurts. Every day, I wish I could ask for her advice about Jeffrey. Just something as simple as, "The baby's got a cold, what should I do?" Oh, sure, I can ask other women with kids, but it's not the same. I want *my* mom to tell me what she did when *I* had a cold. Did she rub my forehead, did she sing a song, and what song did she sing? I want to pass on that tradition, and I can't.

I see mothers and their grown daughters shopping, and I'm envious. They're chatting and laughing, and they have moved beyond the teenage years. I didn't get that chance to share my "mature" self with my mom. A few older women have taken me under their wings. They say, "I'm Sherri's second mom." While I appreciate them so much, it ain't the same. I want my first mom.

Sometimes I get angry, wondering how long she would have lived if she'd taken care of herself. She wasn't very disciplined about insulin shots, and she ate terribly. I guess she didn't think she was worth the effort. My sisters and I respectfully disagree.

> *So write yourself a permission slip to be a little selfish. Insist you take care of your health so you can be around to yell at your kids when they're older. You don't want to miss out on shouting things like, "You are not leaving the house wearing that."*

Fear of a white coat

Compared with whites, blacks and Hispanics have higher rates of diabetes, and lower rates of going to the doctor. Maybe it's because fewer of us have health insurance. Perhaps there's a cultural mistrust of the medical profession. We do not want anyone taking away our food.

And as an African American, I can testify that we eat the wrong foods. We love our fried stuff, our starchy stuff, our sauces, butter, and syrups. Even after a diagnosis, it's hard to give up the foods we grew up with. My own doctor told me, "I don't know what it is about white people, they hear they got diabetes and they start running up hills and hiking up mountains."

Black folks, we love our ribs. They are like a member of the family. We practically have portraits of ribs hanging in our living rooms, we love them so much. If I could have a plate of ribs walk me down the aisle, I would get remarried tomorrow. Giving up pork was hard. A couple of times, I saw the Ghost of Jeffrey Future hovering over me in the meat department.

Whatever works. I may slack off when taking care of myself, but I am a mother lion when it comes to my cub.

> *Write yourself a slip to use any reason that works so you can get healthy. Your kids, your dog, your DVD collection. Somebody or something needs you.*

Finding a vein . . . for my son

I am not a needle person. I could cut out the food, but I had the darndest time sticking myself with a needle. For the first seven months, I avoided the needle, which was unwise. We diabetics need to check our blood sugar three or four times a day, at every meal.

I would stand in the kitchen for a solid hour, looking at my finger, then looking at that needle. Finger. Needle. Finger. Needle. Pork. Ribs. Whoa—pork ribs, what are you doing here? Get away!

Man, it was hard. I was able to stick myself when I was trying to get pregnant, but I was doing it for the baby. Now I was living alone in New York. My son was with his dad in L.A. Without Jeffrey present to guilt me into doing the right thing, I decided to just go by how I felt. My doctor wanted to strangle me. Then Jeffrey came to live with me. That little face changed everything. There I was, in the kitchen. Needle. Finger. Needle. Finger. Jeffrey. Where did Mommy go? Needle. In my finger. Ouch. Done.

Now I do it three or four times a day, like I'm supposed to. And instead of avoiding my doctors, I've got them all on speed dial. If I feel a tingle, I punch 7 to speak to my podiatrist.

"Am I gonna lose my toes? 'Cause I found a great pair of Prada shoes, but I ain't gonna waste my money if they're gonna be too big in a few months."

"Not yet."

That's the killer. I never hear no. Just "not yet."

My doctor was blunt. "If you eat right and exercise, you can stave it off, put it off for a long time, but eventually it's going to happen."

So basically, if I live long enough, I will lose some of my limbs. In fact, the only way I can dodge an amputation is to get hit by a bus on the way to the surgery. And with my luck, the bus would probably run over my good foot.

That's why I always yell at people who tell me they are prediabetic. When you are in that state, *you can still turn the* Titanic *around.* You do not have to crash into that iceberg. All you have to do is cut back on some foods. When you're "pre," you can eat *anything* in moderation, without damaging your body. But once you cross over, those same foods will kill you. There is no bacon when you are diabetic, just turkey bacon. Which is not even bacon at all.

Are you a "pre"? Feeling fine, not worrying about the future? Try this: Fry up some turkey bacon in cooking spray and see how tasty that is. Do a blind taste test with a piece of cardboard and see if you can tell the difference. Imagine eating that for breakfast every day for the rest of your life. Now tell me you can't cut back a little bit.

Diabetes, she is a vampire

I keep my weight down, so inevitably people tell me, "Oh, you don't look diabetic."

I feel it.

Even on my thinnest days, I don't have enough energy. Days when my food is perfect, when I'm eating vegetables—those days should be my best days. Yet even then I don't have *complete* clarity. I feel fuzzy. Not bad, but not good. It's kind of like having a touch of flu, all the time. Except you won't be back to your old self next week. You'll be slightly under the weather, *indefinitely*.

Change course while you can. Start walking. Take a flight of stairs instead of the elevator. Shove a ThighMaster between your legs. For every Pepsi you drink, have two glasses of water. Take baby steps, and you could remain a "pre" for the rest of your life.

> *Write yourself a permission slip to see the doctor once this year. So you don't have to see the doctor every month next year.*

Sherri, if diabetes sucks, why are you always smiling?

Addictable isn't a word, but if it was, I would apply it to me.

I don't handle stress well. When painful feelings threaten to take me down, I tune out. From my teens to my late thirties, I used food, sex, manufactured drama—anything to keep from feeling pain. I was never a big drinker because I was afraid that I'd take a liking to it. Anyone who can get addicted to Cheez Doodles ought to steer clear of tequila. Several of my family members had been addicted to drugs and/or alcohol. There's something about us Shepherds. We have to stay vigilant.

I can say no to drugs and alcohol by keeping them out of the house. But food? You can't go cold turkey off food, no pun intended. In 12-step programs, they liken your addiction to a tiger that needs to be caged. But a food addict has to let the tiger out of its cage three times a day. And put it back each time before a pizza gets devoured. If I didn't have diabetes, the cage would be empty and the tiger would be staying in my bedroom while I slept on the couch.

Diabetes was the only thing that kept me sane for a while. I was experiencing stress that brought me to my knees, in prayer and agony, nearly every day. In fact, if I didn't have diabetes, I would weigh almost four hundred pounds right now. I am not exaggerating, I actually did the math.

When I started on *The View*, I was 187 pounds. On my third day, I had a brain fart and told the world I thought the earth was flat. After you read a few hundred message boards about how dumb you are—that's good for about twenty-five pounds' worth of bingeing.

187 + 25 = 212 lbs.

Now let's throw in two months of flying back and forth to L.A. *every weekend* to visit my son. I'll guess that's another twenty-five pounds.

212 + 25 = 237 lbs.

Add in the moment that I realized that I was too angry to reconcile with my husband, so I decided it was time to divorce. Thirty-five pounds.

237 + 35 = 272 lbs.

Fighting for custody of Jeffrey, fifteen pounds.

272 + 15 = 287 lbs.

Moving to a new city where I barely knew anyone and was too shy to leave my apartment? Seventy-five pounds.

287 + 75 = 362 lbs.

And that's not including the stress of writing this book. Forty pounds.

362 + 40 = 402 lbs.

That's why I thank God for giving me diabetes. I can fit into size 6 jeans. If I was cured of diabetes, which meant that the *only* side effect from overeating was getting fat, I'd drive straight to a McDonald's and order ten number 6s. With a regular Coke, not diet. A Coke so regular that the sugar chunks would get caught in the straw and I'd have to take off the lid and drink from the cup. I would get fatter than fat. I have been good for so long, there would be no stopping me. Grocery stores within a one-mile radius of my home would have to hire armed security guards. Ice cream would have to be delivered by Brinks, because I would be out of my mind.

Can you tell I've been fantasizing lately?

> *If this sounds anything like you, write yourself a permission slip to be grateful for the boundaries you've been given, not resentful. I know this one sounds cheesy, but hey, I wrote myself a slip to be cheesy sometimes, so it's cool.*

Post-diabetes eating is as fun as cleaning the toilet with a toothbrush

I wasn't a fat kid, but I was plump. Cute plump. Like one of those cherubs you see in Renaissance paintings, with pinchable cheeks. Like most women, I always wanted to be thinner. I'd go on Jenny Craig, buy all the Jenny Craig foods, and then binge on all the Jenny Craig desserts. And let me tell you—seven diet desserts don't taste half as good as one regular dessert.

Diabetes forced me to see food as fuel, which is no fun, no fun at all. But most things in life that are good for you are dull like that. One feeling I miss about my old food is how thrilling it was to eat. Face it, eating an ice cream sundae feels dirty. Your heart beats a little faster, you hope no one you know catches you. It's exciting, like cheating on a man you don't really love anymore.

That feeling is gone.

Bad girls don't eat steamed vegetables. When I sit down to a meal now, I'm not going to be transported to another place. I'm gonna have broiled salmon and a salad. And for dessert, maybe an apple. An *apple*. And it's not even in a pie or fritter. Sometimes having diabetes feels like being put in witness protection. I gave up my old friends and past associations, like cheesecake, so I could stay out of the prison also known as the hospital.

I miss my old friends. When I go to a restaurant with my girlfriends, I gotta lay down the ground rule to our waiter: No bread. Then I order a few bottles of their finest Perrier. I can't justify cheating. If I was only worried about gaining weight, I could tell myself, *I'll have some bread and do an extra mile on the treadmill tomorrow.* But I can't compensate for bad foods. That piece of bread tonight could mean a lost toe tomorrow. I gotta make water taste like a white Zinfandel. That's why I order the fancy stuff, like Perrier. I need *something* to come out of a bottle.

I'm definitely not as much fun anymore. My girlfriends will be chatting . . . chowing down appetizers and buzzing on wine. Meanwhile, I'm looking at my watch and motioning for the waiter.

"I'm ready to order. I'll have chicken and a salad."

I'll try to make my baked chicken with lemon last as long as their ribs, and just when I think we're done . . . dang if all my friends want to order dessert. Then I'm back to yelling at the waiter, "Hey, bring out another salad with that dessert tray."

I can hardly concentrate on the conversation. I'm just watching everyone but me shovel pie in their mouths, asking when we can leave. Heck, I'm getting all worked up right now, just writing about it!

All you "pre"s who are reading this book right now? I want you to rent a movie tonight. Something scary: *Nightmare on Elm Street, Jaws,* one of the *Saw*s. Now every time something terrifying happens and you instinctively reach for some popcorn, take a sip of water instead. 'Cause that's your buttered popcorn when you're diabetic. Water.

Okay, I feel better now. Just had to get that off my chest. Sometimes, I think my food plan is gonna make me crazy. New York City is a foodie paradise, like a culinary Sodom and Gomorrah. As soon as I leave my apartment, I have to avert my eyes. There's a pastry shop, a deli, a bagel shop, all open twenty-four hours a day, calling to me, begging me to stop by and pick something up. Or *they deliver*. It's like being the Dalai Lama in the Playboy Mansion. I'm always praying, *Lord, please just help me get to work without an incident.*

At least in Los Angeles, you have to drive somewhere to binge properly. In New York, all you have to do is go for a walk. One time, in the throes of my Pinkberry obsession, I seriously contemplated leaving my sleeping son alone in the apartment, because a Pinkberry run was ten minutes, round trip.

I can imagine explaining to Child Protective Services why Jeffrey's mom wasn't home when the building caught on fire.

"I just wanted a medium!"

> *Write yourself a permission slip to stop pretending you don't mind if someone orders the food equivalent of a coma, right in front of you. And then make them pick up the check.*

People avoid feelings for a reason

Food anesthetized me for so long that when I couldn't "use" anymore, I was practically in shock. Not only was I feeling deep emotional pain, but I was feeling it, raw, for the first time. If you have open-heart surgery, you expect to be sore after you wake up. But you don't expect to be conscious while the surgeon is cutting you open.

That's what it feels like to get a divorce, without ribs.

Diabetes forces me to be *present* in my feelings. And while therapists will tell you that being *present* is optimum, I will tell you that being present is highly overrated. You can't escape anything. Listen, there's a good reason that human beings get addicted to anything under the sun—feelings hurt. Being alive is painful.

Unfortunately, "the sugar" leaves me no other option.

Present people make the worst neighbors in the world. There's times where I sit on the floor in the middle of my living room and howl like a shot bear. When I sob, I make the same noise an animal makes when he dies, "Mawrrrrrrrrrrrrrrrr!" I'm surprised no one's complained to Animal Control. "The lady next door to me is hunting grizzlies in her kitchen. Hurry!"

Like I've said, I believe that God gives you a hole so you can fill it with Him. However, potato chips work a lot faster. And that lag time, from when that hole is torn open to when God mosies on over to heal it . . . oh boy. That's when you gotta be present. Just sit there, and wait for that knock on your soul:

"Sherri, it's Me. Can I come in?"

"YES! HURRY!"

When I see addicts who cannot kick their habit, I understand. Those moments when you're waiting for grace, they are genuine agony. A desire becomes a part of your body, like a bone, and almost impossible to deny. One M&M becomes three, then six, then the bag, then what the hell, I'm going to Pinkberry. Being present means you hang on to the edge of that cliff until God pulls you up. You don't let go, no matter how much your fingers hurt, no matter how badly you'd rather fall.

I've been Dumpster-diving in my own home, pulling out pieces of garbage that were covering the food I threw away. Food I should've flushed. Food I didn't flush because part of me knew I'd want to eat it later, even if it had been in the trash. If a food plan told me I could have ten chips, I'd eat ten on the way to the couch, ten at the couch, and ten on the way back to the pantry. Then I'd make about eight more round trips . . . until I finished the bag.

In fact, right after I had Jeffrey, I ate my way up to 197 pounds. I almost fainted when I saw that number on the scale. Because two hundred pounds was my freak-out number. Something about that milestone was horrifying to me, like once I'd crossed that river, I wasn't going back. It was on to Rome.

That's when I tried the Master Cleanse for fifteen days. I read that Beyoncé did it for *Dreamgirls,* and that was good enough for me. But of course, I gained back most of what I lost. Once a girlfriend told me to drink apple cider, vinegar, and hot water, because then I would pee fat. Literally, urinate my fat cells. It sounded fishy, but when you're desperate, you'll try anything. In the end, years of crash and crazy dieting slowed down my metabolism.

And then the diabetes moved in and did the rest.

I don't engage in life-threatening binges anymore, but some days my food is better than others. When I eat my veggies, I feel decent and my mind is clear. When I don't, I feel worse and my thinking is foggy. It's pretty simple and unbelievably hard.

> *Write yourself a permission slip to ask*
> *God to help you when you're weak. You*
> *don't have to do it all. In fact, you can't,*
> *so you might as well get the best help*
> *available.*

Like mother, like son

"Mommy," says Jeffrey as we walk by a bakery, "cookie."

"No. No cookie."

He cries, I fold my arms, and that's that. This conversation happens at least once a week, and it's only going to get worse when he learns to pronounce *Frappuccino*.

My son is genetically predisposed to get diabetes. The doctor didn't tell me this, my family tree did. My mom and my grandparents were not educated about nutrition. I probably have other ancestors who died from complications of diabetes, like a stroke or high blood pressure, but no one put two and two together. I want to be the last Shepherd who becomes diabetic. I want our awful legacy to stop with me.

More and more children in this country are diabetic. Why? Is it our lifestyle, or the additives in food? The corn syrup, sucrose, dextrose, anything that ends with *ose* plus a whole bunch of stuff I can't pronounce. Fruits and vegetables are more expensive than a Happy Meal. All I know is kids should be playing tag and calling each other "it," not sticking themselves with needles.

I have Type 2, which means I'm supposed to be on medication.

But Type 1 diabetes means insulin injections, and that's a whole other level of commitment. I use a needle to check my blood. I shouldn't skip a blood test, but I can. It's not recommended, but I can get away with it. If you need insulin, though—that's injecting yourself, every day, like clockwork. You cannot blow it off, not once. How many times have you seen some sort of bank hostage drama on Lifetime, and the diabetic hostage goes into shock because he can't get to his insulin? That's the kind of crap a Type 1 diabetic has to worry about every day.

Skip the rest of this paragraph if you are not a "pre." Okay, it's just us sugar heads here? Good. GO TO THE DOCTOR, TAKE CARE OF YOURSELF BEFORE IT'S TOO LATE. I'm sorry. I know all-caps is considered shouting, and that's what I'm doing. Shouting. Because some of y'all have thick skulls. Don't wait until God gives you a vision of your kid asking where Heaven is because that's where Mommy lives. Sheesh.

Dancing my life away at Club Diabetes

Now that I'm a charter member, I try to make the best of my situation. My change in diet was abrupt. I went from cupcakes, pancakes—okay, all cakes—to salmon grilled in . . . nothing. It was like someone put my taste buds in solitary confinement. They had nothing to do, no one to talk to. My mouth was slowly going mad. I started trolling diabetes Web sites, newsgroups, looking for ways to make healthy food taste unhealthy, dirty again. I had to find a way to fake my old lifestyle.

That's when I turned on to the sugar-free world.

I never ate low-calorie foods. I was uninterested in any food that started with *Diet, Lite, Lean,* or *Healthy.* Unless I was on a diet, which only lasted until I cheated. And anything that started with *Sugar* but ended with *Free* was a definite "no thank you." If I picked up a carton of ice cream and noticed it said *Sugar Free,* I would drop it like it was contagious. As if it would make *me* sugar free. Then I'd start looking for the sugar-full ice cream. 'Cause they gotta stick that freed sugar somewhere.

Usually when you join a club, there's a hazing process, some kind of physical torture. That's how I look on my experience with sugar-free candy. Violent. Painful. Like a gang initiation.

Some genius heard about the soaring diabetes rates in the United States and decided to market an entire line of candy for people who can't eat candy. This person makes sugar-free versions of everything I like to eat. Sugar-free peanut butter cups. Sugar-free Snickers-type bars. Sugar-free Pixy Stix.

I was so excited when I found the catalog. I bought enough candy for a hundred Halloweens. *Oh, God, how do they do it,* I wondered.

I would find out.

These foods substitute sugar with malatol, which makes your blood sugar rise very slowly. *Great,* I thought, *I can eat as much as I want. It's like not having diabetes at all. Hallelujah.* The first peanut butter cup tasted great. Not like grilled salmon at all. I finished off the bag. I wasn't worried, because the malatol would keep me on an even keel.

Well, not all of me.

One of malatol's side effects is diarrhea. Take my word for it, anytime a warning label says, "May cause diarrhea," it means, "Will cause diarrhea." And you need to plan for that. Stay home. Have access to a bathroom. One you don't have to share with a loved one. If you know you're gonna be in for the night—you have a test to study for, or you already have diarrhea anyway—then rip open a bag of sugar-free candy and have at it.

Otherwise, stay clear.

Do not binge on sugar-free products before a baby shower, a night out at a club, or a flight. Once I was on a plane and I felt some "side effects" coming. We were all buckled in and I couldn't get to the bathroom in time. The side effects soiled my pants.

That was my last sugar-free binge.

Call me old-fashioned, but I think stools should be firm. As much as I loved the taste of sugar-free sweets, I couldn't make that commitment to the bathroom. I had to let those treats go and return to my strict, boring, healthy diet.

Now my tolerance for sugar is so low, I can't even cheat when I try. I took a vacation to Costa Rica, and food was included in the package. Well, there I was in a tropical paradise. Being a good girl. Eating my veggies, ordering my fish un-fried, surrounded by my buzzed, happy friends. Me staring at their food, me glaring at their colorful drinks, me ordering steamed cauliflower and bottled water. I lasted for three days. Then I lost my way.

"This mess is for the birds," I said. "They ain't gonna cut off my foot in Costa Rica."

"Sherri, don't do it!" said one of my girlfriends.

"I'll have a piña colada!" I told a waiter. I convinced myself that I forgot to pack my diabetes—it was on the kitchen counter where I left it.

I drank my drink and jumped in the pool. The sugar hit my blood at the same time the water hit my skin. Whoosh. I slid under the water, then popped back up.

"Hey," I shouted, "I'm dying. I mean . . . I'm going under in this pool right now. Bye!"

I didn't seem to mind that I was a goner. Sugar will kill you and make you smile while she does it. My friends jumped in and pulled me from the pool.

No more piñas.

So even though I look pretty darn good in a swimsuit, I can't lounge around the pool, sipping umbrella drinks. At least I'm in good company. Halle Berry has diabetes, and so does Randy Jackson. I love to meet other diabetics on *The View*.

"You're a needle freak? Me too!"

It's like having a friend for life.

As I write this book, I am the same age as my mother was when she died. Part of me was always worried that I wouldn't get older than her, that I was doomed to inherit her time line. But our luck changed. Or maybe I changed it. I'm in good health and the odds are good that I'll walk my son down the aisle, meddle in his marriage, and interfere with how he raises my grandchildren. If we're really lucky, I'll be the last Shepherd with diabetes. And generations from now, my descendants can read about how Granny Sherri had to walk to school, uphill both ways, carrying a pack of syringes.

> *So write yourself a permission slip to be the first in your family to do something, or the first not to.*

part seven

Permission to Have a Less-Than-Perfect Family

My sisters live in Los Angeles, my dad lives in Chicago, and I live in New York, yet somehow we're close. Among the three of us girls, we've given my dad seven grandchildren and one ex-son-in-law. If this was a 1940s movie, right about now I'd cue the dream-sequence/flashback special effects, and the announcer would say:

"It all started about nine months before little Sherri's birth date, April 22, 1967 . . ."

A sperm meets an egg

My mother was a very quiet, refined young woman. A lady. (No, I was not adopted.) Mom aspired to be a doctor, which was a pretty big dream for a black girl growing up in Chicago's Southside projects in the 1960s.

Then she met my dad.

Dad was, and is, a charmer. The consummate salesman. He can sell ice to an Eskimo who sells ice to other Eskimos. He's *that* good. He could charm the pants off, well, my mom. And he did.

Mom lost her virginity on the same night she got pregnant with me. She was the original multitasker. Back in those days, you either got married or gave the baby up. So my parents had a traditional (as in shotgun) wedding. And instead of going to medical school, LaVerne Shepherd became a wife and mother. She was from that last generation of women who weren't encouraged to do both.

Of course it takes two to get pregnant, but my mother was so shy and proper that I completely blame my dad. Mom had five siblings and she took care of them all. They were poor, and her life was not remotely glamorous. Then along comes Lawrence Shepherd, with his booming voice, outgoing personality, and jokes. She probably thought, *Is this guy for real?* And five minutes later, she was pregnant.

Like my mom, Dad was of his generation, too.

"I put you in this situation, LaVerne," he told her. "You're carrying my baby, I'm going to marry you."

He, too, set aside his dreams to provide for his daughter. He wanted to be in show business, but he joined the service and got stationed in Okinawa, Japan. When he came back for his first leave, my sister Lisa was conceived.

Stealing my thunder

I have two sisters, Lisa and Lauren (Lori). Lauren is seven years younger than me—the baby. I'll save her for later. Lisa is two years younger, but from birth has acted like she was ten years older. Lisa is outspoken where I am shy, and she will fight when I would prefer to run to the nearest police station.

Once, at a large Jehovah's Witnesses Assembly, my family got to the arena early. My mother decided to save some seats for other Brothers and Sisters from our Kingdom Hall. She left to get a snack, assigning me to watch over the saved seats.

"Sherri, don't let anybody sit here, I'll be right back."

"Mama, I don't want to tell grown-ups what to do!" I said. I was nine years old. Confrontation was not my style.

"It's not *telling* people what to do, it's *explaining* that your mother has saved seats for fellow Witnesses."

"But I don't—"

"You'll be fine," she said, and she left.

Naturally, as soon as she walked away, a group of grown-ups spotted our empty row. They started calling over their people.

"Oh hey! Y'all! Come here! Here's some chairs!"

I stood there, watching, as they placed their Bibles on the seats my mother had reserved for all her friends. They congratulated themselves on finding such good seats.

"You can't let nobody sit there," Lisa whispered. "Mama told you to say something."

"What do you want me to do?" I said. "These are grown-ups. I can't do it."

Lisa, who was seven, stood up and marched over to whoever seemed like their leader.

"Excuse me, you can't sit there. My mama said nobody can sit in these seats."

I thought Lisa would get yelled at, but these folks chuckled, gathered their Bibles, and left. Wow. My little sister was cool.

The Moose gets loose

Lisa was always ready to rumble. She would fight you verbally or physically, whichever worked best. I preferred to joke my way out of situations. Since both my parents grew up in the projects, they believed it was important to stand up for yourself. If either of them found out that we'd run from a fight, they would put us in the car and drive us straight to the person's house.

Even though we bickered, Lisa saved me from a beatdown in an after-school girlfight. I was in third grade. There was a girl in my class who was at least twice my height. I can't remember her name, so I'll call her Moose.

Moose had been held back several times—in fact, I'm pretty sure she had her driver's license. Maybe even a husband and kids. She'd been giving me the evil eye because I had long hair that Mom braided. My braids hung down my back, long and pretty, and I guess Moose didn't like that.

"I'm gonna beat you up," she said.

At our school, if you wanted to fight a girl, you announced it to her face. It was a courtesy to the other kids, so they could rearrange their schedules and watch.

That day, Lisa and I started walking home. I heard Moose call.

"Hey, Sherri! You better turn around! I'm going to beat you up!"

My dad had always taught us to stand our ground. "Shepherds don't run." That was his mantra, and it played over and over again in my head as I stood there, paralyzed with fear, wondering why my legs wouldn't move. *Maybe that's why Shepherds don't run. We can't.* A huge crowd of kids had gathered behind us. Moose was so much taller than me that I could only see one of her eyes. She looked like a Cyclops.

As Moose came toward me, I found my legs. I kicked her, karate-style, hard in her stomach. And while Moose didn't fall, I did. As I staggered up, she punched me in the face.

The crowd went insane with pure, elementary school bloodlust.

"Fight! Fight! Fight!" they chanted.

Moose took their advice and began to whale on me. I saw stars. Just when I thought I couldn't stand any more, I heard a banshee-like scream.

"Aaaaaiiiiiiii!"

It was my little sister Lisa. She burst through the circle of kids and jumped on Moose's back. Climbed right up Moose's body like a Polynesian boy scaling a coconut tree. When Lisa got to the top, she bit Moose, hard.

"Aaaaaaaaah!" Moose screamed.

Moose tried to shake Lisa off, but Lisa hung on, like a pit bull.

"Don't mess with my sister!" she screamed, unclenching her jaw. Then my little sister finished Moose off. She grabbed my hand and walked us through the kids. She was spitting out chunks of Moose's back the whole way home.

And Moose left me alone after that. Didn't say boo. In fact, saving me from Moose is the only thing that saved Lisa a few years later after she told my mom that I had lost my virginity. Otherwise, I would've found the strength to kill her.

Little sisters . . . sometimes they save you, sometimes they snitch on you.

> *Sound familiar? If so, write your sister a permission slip and tell her she's off the hook for one crappy thing she did. (But just one. You might need the others for potential blackmail purposes.)*

Whuppin'

My parents used to whup us. Before you go calling Child Protective Services on my dad, let me explain the concept of a "whuppin'." (Black folks, skip ahead, I know you know what I'm talking about.) Whuppin's do not involve whips. In fact, all you need for a successful whuppin' is a hand, a knee, and a clothed bottom. And some love. A whuppin' is *always* delivered with love. In fact, good parents remind their children of this fact during the whuppin' procedure.

"I'm."

SMACK.

"Doing."

SMACK.

"This."

SMACK.

"Because."

SMACK.

"I."

SMACK.

"Love."

SMACK.

"You."

KISS. HUG. SNUGGLE.

This logic doesn't make sense until you become a parent. When you have to deliver a whuppin' to a child who is otherwise unable to stop himself from sipping Drano or telling big Auntie Faith that Daddy calls her "Auntie Fat," then you understand.

I used to get whupped for getting home from school late. We were classic 1970s latchkey kids; both my parents worked. School got out at two forty-five, and our house was fifteen minutes away by foot. My parents factored in an extra fifteen minutes for horsing around, and expected us to be home at three fifteen. Dad would call the house from work at exactly three fifteen.

And if we didn't answer the phone? Whuppin'.

He didn't care if we had a great excuse.

"Sherri, it's three sixteen. How come you're late?"

"It's just a minute!"

"Where were you?"

"At the park. They cleaned the swings!"

"Sherri, you and your sister—"

"But Daddy, we was on the slide!"

"—are gonna get a whuppin' when I get home."

Miss Crockett

"I'm going to tell your father when he gets home."

Those are ten words a child never wants to hear. Basically, they mean that Mom is too tired to administer a whuppin', so she's passing the baton to Dad, who will be fresh and ready to whup when he gets home from work.

In fourth grade, someone dared me to tell a teacher to shut up. I always took on nonphysical dares. When I play "Truth or Dare," it's just called "Truth." I always figured, *Why use my fists when I can get in as much trouble with my mouth?*

My girlfriends and I were walking up some stairs.

"Do it, Sherri. Please! You'll be my hero forever."

Well, that was all I needed. I leaned over the railing.

"Shut up, Miss Crockett."

Then I ran. I sprinted up the stairs and ducked into a classroom. Miss Crockett was fast on my heels and found me. It was like she'd been taking lessons from my mother.

"I'm telling your father, Sherri Shepherd," she panted. "I'm going to call him right now."

Oh boy. I sat in class with a sick feeling in my stomach, imagining Dad leaving McDonald's, getting in the car, each stoplight making him angrier. After a few minutes, a teacher poked her head in my class.

"Mr. Shepherd is here for his daughter."

I met my dad in the hallway. Miss Crockett was standing next to him, frowning. She had stopped panting.

"Sherri. Did you tell Miss Crockett to shut up?" he asked.

"Yes, sir."

Nobody even gave me credit for calling her "Miss Crockett." I could've said "Shut up, old hag." But instead, I kept it respectful. I decided to keep this defense to myself.

"And what would you like to do right now?" Dad asked.

Run away, I thought.

"Apologize, sir."

"That's what I thought."

I took in a breath and said it as fast as I could.

"MissCrockettI'msorryfortellingyoutoshutup."

"Thank you, Sherri, I accept your apology," said Miss Crockett.

She walked away. Dad stood there, arms folded.

"Daddy, am I gonna get a whuppin'?"

"Yup. I'll see you tonight." He kissed me on the forehead and returned to McDonald's.

Well, at least I got some notice.

The baby always gets away with murder

Lisa and I got whupped so much that by the time Lauren was born, my parents were too tired to give her the business. Except once.

At the beginning of every school year, my parents would buy me a special three-ring notebook. And my second-grade notebook was amazing. It was covered in denim, and it looked like a pair of Dittos jeans. I loved my notebook. I couldn't wait for school to start so I could hold it to my chest and prance down the hall. I carefully printed my name in the inside, and my phone number. "If returned," I reminded potential thieves, "no questions will be asked."

School started the next day. I laid my denim notebook carefully on the table, next to my crayons. I went into the kitchen. About a minute later, Lauren, who was one, waddled by me. She was grinning and waving one of my crayons. The orange crayon.

You probably know what happened next.

"AAAAAH," I screamed.

My parents came running, Lauren came crawling. I don't remember where Lisa was, but she was probably laughing.

"DADDY!" I shouted. "LAUREN DREW ALL OVER MY NOTEBOOK!"

"Calm down, girl. How do you know it was Lauren?"

I pointed to Exhibits A—my denim notebook, which was covered in orange scribbles; and B—Lauren, who was chewing on an orange crayon.

"Daddy, stop her, she's eating the evidence!"

Dad pulled the crayon out of Lauren's mouth, pointed to the notebook, and said, "No."

Then he let her go. I was appalled.

"Daddy, you supposed to whup her!"

"You want me to whup a one-year-old?"

"HARD!"

Daddy lifted up Lauren and gave her a few swats on the behind. I wasn't satisfied.

"Daddy, that ain't good enough! She ain't even crying. Let me do it!"

I grabbed Lauren and tried to bend her over my knee.

"Sherri Shepherd, put your sister down! You wanna be next?"

Dang!

Now, as a Christian, I don't believe in reincarnation, but if I'm wrong, I want to come back as the baby in the family. 'Cause they get away with *everything*.

> *So write yourself a permission slip to give one spanking. Because you know you will at some point, and your child will survive. (Of course, the spanking doesn't have to be given to your child . . .)*

Opposites repel

My parents did not get along.

What probably would have been a two-month fling in high school turned into sixteen years of fighting, because they wanted to do right by their children. Growing up, I identified more with my father, probably because we're so similar. Mom thought he was too loud, too flirty, and too irreverent. Which are exactly the things I love best about him.

Mom was hard to please. Once she threw him a surprise birthday party. She managed to hide about thirty people in the house. Someone said, "Shhh, he's home!"

And we all hushed up, listening to my dad walk up the steps. But I couldn't help myself. I was five, and excited. I peeked through the window and waved to him. He saw me, and waved back.

When he came in, everyone yelled "Surprise!" and my dad seemed surprised. But my mom thought I'd ruined it.

She took me aside and chewed me out. I ran upstairs, crying, and crawled under my bed. I heard my dad clomp up the stairs after me. He pulled me out from under the bed and held me in his arms.

"It's all right, Sherri. I was surprised. I swear I didn't even know."

I don't know if he was telling the truth or just making me feel better, but it worked. Even now, there are times I just want to crawl under my bed and cry. And if I call my dad, he'll say the same thing, with the same voice.

"It's all right, Sherri, it's all right."

And it always is.

Southside living

Before we moved to the 'burbs, we lived in the Southside. In the 1970s, Chicago's Southside was as black as its suburbs were white. We knew everybody, and everybody knew us. It was friendly like that. Dad was popular—he used to throw house parties in our basement. I guess now the term *house party* brings to mind some brat teenager letting his friends trash his home while his parents are on vacation. But back in the day, a house party was a thing the grown-ups had.

My sisters and I loved watching the adults make fools of themselves. Dad would buy some cheap booze—Champale or Boone's Farm—and play DJ for the night. He had a record player, and tons of albums in a box. Dad would put on the Ohio Players and Gladys Knight and the grown-ups would start doing the Hustle or the Funky Chicken.

All this revelry went down in the Shepherd family basement, which was a thing to behold. It was classic 1970s tacky. The decor was the height of fashion at the time, but if you saw it now, your eyes would bleed. On one wall was a painting of a black man and woman. They had giant Afros, they were hugging, and they were completely naked. That was our "black power" wall. Across the room was a velvet painting of a bullfighter and a bull. That was the "Shepherds don't run" wall. On the third wall, my dad hung a giant wooden fork and spoon. I could never figure out the artistic intention behind oversize flatware, but people always commented on it.

"Lawrence, that's quite a fork."

"I know, I know. Don't forget to check out the spoon."

The fourth wall was covered floor-to-ceiling in scenic wallpaper. It was a forest, with a dozen life-size trees and trunks. If you were a guest at Dad's house party, theoretically you could get drunk enough to think you had stumbled upon the mythical Southside Forest. A deep, dark woods where, behind you, unicorns were dancing to "The Night the Lights Went Out in Georgia."

Oh, you think I'm finished? I haven't even described the plug-in water fountain. When you switched on the waterfall, the rocks lit up red.

In general, my mother was not a fan of the house parties. She let my dad have them, but I never saw her Hustle or Slide. She'd just sit on the couch, sipping her Boone's. Keeping a quiet eye on her stuff, her man, her children.

Everyone knows everyone

When I was an actress in L.A., my grandmother used to tell me to look up a boy I grew up with.

"Sherri, you got to go see Ms. Jones's grandbaby! He out there in Hollywood and he out there doing that acting, too."

Those were all the clues I got, but she kept nagging me.

"Sherri, Ms. Jones's *grandbaby*, Michael. You remember him. He lives out there in Hollywood. You gotta go see him."

Of course, I did not look up this Jones kid. However, when I was working on *Less Than Perfect*, actor Michael Boatman from *Spin City* was doing a guest role. We got to chatting. Turns out we were both from Chicago, both from the Southside. Then Michael mentioned his grandmother, Miss Jones.

"Oh, my God!" I said. "Did you know my grandmother, Mrs. Shepherd?"

"Mrs. Shepherd was your grandmother? I used to stop by and see her little granddaughter."

"THAT WAS ME!"

So after a few more stories, I realized it was Michael who'd stepped in when I was a little girl to help me fend off some boys. He got beat up for it. So, Michael Boatman, I owe you one.

Movin' on up . . . to Hoffman Estates

Dad moved us to the suburbs when I was eleven. We moved in the middle of the week that *Roots* first aired, and we were very careful not to miss a night. Back then, of course, if you missed an episode, you had to wait until the network reran it. My parents wanted us to grow up in a safe place, and the Southside was dangerous. They really busted their behinds to make that happen.

Dad worked three jobs, while my mom cleaned houses and sold art.

One of Dad's part-time jobs was waiting tables at a Sambo's, a restaurant chain whose icon was a black baby with giant red lips. I didn't realize how offensive that image was, I just knew I'd never seen a black infant who looked remotely like the Sambo baby. I thought it was dumb.

Dad was a popular waiter, yet he experienced blatant racism. People called him the N-word, to his face, almost every day. I'm not being negative, but this was a very white suburb in the 1970s, and that's what happened. Yet some people would wait extra long so they could sit at Larry Shepherd's table, because he made your meal fun.

Dad put up with it because he wanted a better life for his girls.

"You just have to go out there and you have to do a great job. You have to be better than everybody else," he told me, many times. He believed that excellence was the best way to outwit racism.

He shielded us from much of it. Many times we would go to a

restaurant for a nice family dinner, and wait. And wait. And wait. Nobody would talk to us, or take our order. Even though he knew exactly what was happening, he wouldn't point it out, because he didn't want us to grow up bitter.

"This is their busy hour," he'd say of the waiters avoiding our table, "they'll get to us when they can."

He worked so hard. After Sambo's closed, Dad started waiting tables at Denny's part-time. I remember how he'd come home with his tips and give the loose change to Lisa and me, so we could learn to save our money. He also worked full-time at Northwest Hospital, managing the cafeteria.

Oh, and he had one other job.

Working girl

I assisted Dad at his third gig, selling Mary Kay Cosmetics.

That's right. My dad was a Mary Kay consultant.

Listen, some people are good at multilevel marketing, and my dad is one of them. If there's a product that can be sold by joining a club and attending meetings, my dad has sold it. Mary Kay, Amway, legal aid, insurance. Once Dad gets on board, he is a true believer.

And my dad loved him some Mary Kay.

If Dad's house parties were great, his Mary Kay parties were phenomenal. He'd let me set up the trays. Each guest had her own tray of cosmetics. Dad was a huge flirt, which helped sales immensely. And he spoke in a deep, Barry White baritone (like God!) that the women *loved*.

"Oh, my goodness, you look absolutely beautiful," he'd say, applying makeup to a woman's face.

"Really?"

"Girl, I gotta remind myself I'm married! Will that be cash or credit?"

Ka-ching.

Blue eye shadow was my dad's specialty. He sold loads of it. Now, you and I know that nobody looks good in blue eye shadow, except maybe Diana Ross. But my dad wasn't lying. He loved the blue eye shadow. The bluer, the better. To this day, he still likes a woman in a nice black dress and a pair of aqua eyelids.

Dad was going for that Mary Kay pink Cadillac. Unfortunately, my mom did not approve of his flirty sales technique and pulled the plug on that gig before Dad had a chance to earn his Caddy.

So he bought one.

It's probably impossible to overstate the importance of the Cadillac brand to a certain type of African American family, and the Shepherds were one of those families. My dad loved Cadillacs. The Coupe DeVille was the cream, and the Sedan DeVille was the crop. And since he couldn't earn the cream, he bought the crop.

Dad's Sedan DeVille came with an eight-track, which, like floor-to-ceiling forest wallpaper, was considered badass in the 1970s. I remember going with my dad to his Thursday softball game. He was playing Chic's "Le Freak," and when he pulled up, all the guys gathered around.

"Aww! Brother! You bad!"

Yes, he was.

> *Write yourself a slip to look back fondly on the goofy parts of your childhood.*

Going against my nature

I didn't have nearly as much fun going to work with my mom. That's because she cleaned houses. On the weekends. So while every other self-respecting eleven-year-old girl was home, playing jump rope and Barbies, there I was, following my mother with a pail of paper towels and Windex. One of her houses had a family with girls my age.

"Sherri, you want to play?" one of them asked.

"Yeah!" I said. One of the sisters had a tea set that was *to die for*.

"Oh, no," said my mother, "Sherri, go clean out that soap dish."

"I don't want to clean that soap dish," I shouted. "I want to go play! They got a tea set!"

Guess who got a whuppin'?

My mom loved cleaning, and she loved the smell of a bleached house. If Lisa or I didn't clean something properly, she'd wake us up in the middle of the night for a do-over. I remember, at age five, vowing to myself that I would never clean my own house.

And one look at my apartment proves I kept that promise to myself. It is a pigsty, or so I'm told. I don't notice, because I don't care. My housekeeping motto is "Carpe Diem." As in, seize the day, and don't waste a second of it scrubbing a dang toilet.

When people visit, I warn them at the door.

"My house is junky. I'll probably clean it in another year. It don't bother you, come on in. If it does, God bless you and keep on moving."

Door-to-door painting sales

My mom also sold art. But not at a craft fair with hippies, like everyone else. No, that's not humiliating enough for the Shepherds.

Instead, Mom and I would take a bunch of canvases to people's homes, lay them out, and hope for a sale. If you wanted a painting of an apple or some animals, and you thought your friends might, too, all you had to do was call the Shepherd girls. We would be right over. Lots of our customers were Jehovah's Witnesses, as we'd joined the Kingdom Hall by then.

Again, I'd go with my mother to work and see kids my age, hanging out on their porches.

"Mom, I didn't sign up for this," I said once, lugging paintings past some kids who were sitting around, doing nothing.

"You want to keep taking that photography class, don't you?"

"I don't need photography class that bad," I said. I was ready to quit if this agony was the price I had to pay.

"Too late," she said, "now get up these stairs and hand me those pictures."

Becoming Witnesses

Mom was never comfortable in Dad's Baptist church. There's a lot going on. Speaking in tongues, running, drumming, and just plenty of Holy Rollering in general. Baptists are very demonstrative, and that didn't sit well with my mom. One day, a Jehovah's Witness came to the house, and everything they offered was exactly what my mother wanted. The Kingdom Hall was very serene. Worshippers listened while a church elder spoke, and if you wanted to say something, you raised your hand. Drums were replaced by a piano, and instead of running up the aisle, you were asked to open a Psalm book to page 119, sing a hymn, and then sit down.

Not surprisingly, the tradition of the Shepherd Family House

Party ended. It was replaced with the Shepherd Family Get-Together. Basically, booze and the Hustle turned into soda and board games. Those nights were fun, but a different kind of fun—a Sorry, Mouse Trap, and Monopoly kind of fun.

I could tell my dad wasn't happy. He converted because he had no choice. Mom basically said, "We're joining the Jehovah's Witnesses and if you don't come with us, I'm leaving you."

When I was older, Dad told me, "I gave up everything I believed in and became a Witness so my wife would not take my kids."

They would divorce six years later, and Mom took his kids, anyway.

Losing my hair, at age seven

They fought a lot on the way to their divorce. When I was about seven, Dad moved out. And he got a girlfriend. Lisa and I met her, and we liked her a lot. She wore a short skirt and white go-go boots. Being kids, we didn't think anything was wrong with telling Mom all about her.

"Mama, Daddy's girlfriend is pretty!"

My mom snapped her neck around with superhero speed.

"Girlfriend?"

"Uh-huh! She pretty!"

"Who is Lawrence with?!"

Looking back, I can see that Mom was preparing to commit murder. All she needed was an address. Of course, when you're seven, you don't pick up on the subtleties of homicidal rage. My mom put Lisa and me in her orange Cutlass Supreme and took us driving through girlfriend-likely neighborhoods.

"Is this what the building looked like?" she asked, in an effort to rule out certain styles of apartment buildings.

"Uh-uh, Mama. That ain't it."

"What about that one?"

"Uh-uh." We thought she wanted to say hi to the lady.

"What about that one?"

"Oh! That's it, Mama!"

Mom pulled over and we started looking around, like Karen Hill outside Janice's apartment in *Goodfellas*. But we had the wrong building. We never found Dad's girlfriend. Thank goodness, because my shy, prim mother was set to beat this lady to death, right in front of her children. (Interestingly enough, thirty-two years later I would make that same drive, looking for *my* husband's girlfriend.)

I missed my dad so much. There was no one to help me with my homework, or take me to church and tell me how pretty I was. Dad used to take me out on little dates, the two of us were like Peas and Carrots. And when Peas moved out, Carrots started going crazy—or as crazy as a seven-year-old can. I started misbehaving in school. And my hair started falling out. I had bald patches all over my little head. One night Dad came over to the house. I was crying. He held me hard.

"Sherri, I'm going to make this promise to you. I will not leave again. I will never leave you, until you can understand. Your mom and I are going to stay together."

I had such a feeling of relief. My hair almost grew back overnight. My dad was home. Yes, they argued all the time, but he was home. I was seventeen when they finally divorced.

> ***Write yourself a permission slip to
> focus on the sacrifices that your parents
> did make, instead of the ones they didn't.***

Moving to L. A.

It was Mom who finally pulled the trigger on the marriage. She took my sisters and me to Los Angeles. She didn't have a job lined up, she just wanted to go someplace warm. Taking two teens and a ten-year-old to Los Angeles was probably the most adventurous thing she ever did, besides marrying my dad.

Lisa and I went nuts now that we were no longer under Dad's thumb. We snuck out, we disobeyed rules. Boys. Boys. Boys. Mom had to get two jobs to pay the rent, so she wasn't home much, and when she was, she was too tired to discipline us.

Even worse, that dang art company Mom worked for in Chicago had a franchise in Los Angeles. But instead of bringing canvases to people's homes, Mom decided to set up shop on a street corner, right near my high school. My job was to sit with her and not die of embarrassment.

"Mom, can't we go somewhere else?" I was the new student. I didn't want the kids to know me as the girl from Chicago who sold animal paintings at the intersection.

"No, this corner gets good traffic. A lot of people pass by this corner," she said.

"Yeah, and I go to school with all of them."

Cars drove by, honked.

"Hey, Sherri!" said a girl whom I thought I recognized from my math class.

"Hey," I said, hoping the earth would open and swallow me alive.

"What you doing?"

"Selling lion paintings. Want one?"

She did not. I helped my mom sell Tupperware, too. In retrospect, all that assisting was good for my character. I learned to be helpful, of service. I would like to pass on those lessons to Jeffrey. I could start selling Amway on the side. Maybe I'll try to sneak a sales pitch in during Hot Topics.

> **Write yourself a permission slip to humiliate your children as you were humiliated. C'mon. Why should they be spared?**

Thank God I had a son, because I deserved to have me as a daughter

My mom was beloved by her clients, too. An attorney whose house she cleaned for years bought her a car after the divorce. I'm hard on my mom, but I give her complete credit for putting up with me. I became a rebellious nightmare when I entered my teens. If someone told me rain was wet, I'd say, "No it ain't! Rain's dry!"

Mom was on the receiving end of most of my anger because, when I was younger, I didn't want my dad to leave us again. And since Mom wasn't going anywhere, I felt secure enough to tell her, once a day, "I hate you and I can't wait till I'm eighteen so I can move out."

At one point, I was ending all my sentences that way.

"What do you want for breakfast, Sherri?"

"Cheerios and I hate you and I can't wait till I'm eighteen so I can move out."

Sneaking out

Like most seventeen-year-olds, I used to sneak out of the house. I'd tell my mom I was babysitting.

"Okay, well, what time you gonna be home?"

"Whenever they get home. I'm not sure."

"Well, what's their phone number?"

"Their phone got turned off."

I would dash out before she could get suspicious, and change clothes in the apartment building laundry room. I went from babysitter to superfreak in five minutes, like Wonder Woman. My friends Yosepha, Earlene, and Angelina would be waiting for me outside.

Back then you could borrow an ID from someone outside, get your hand stamped, and give it back to them. And since bouncers barely checked, you didn't have to find anyone who looked remotely like you. I probably could've used a white girl's ID. "Yeah, that's me, so what?"

Ah, those were the days, my friends. We'd go to strip clubs and just get wild. One night, I came home, and someone had stolen my "babysitter" clothes, which I always stashed in the bushes next to the laundry room. I ran back to Yosepha's car.

"What am I gonna do? This is my mother's top. I can't walk into the house wearing my mother's good blouse. She'll kill me!"

"Here, take mine." Yosepha took off her oversize shirt. I opened the front door, expecting to be yelled at. And Mom was waiting for me, but she had fallen asleep. I crept by, feeling lucky.

Some incredibly juicy blind-item gossip

The four of us were a dangerous quartet. Yosepha and Earlene were beautiful and looked way older than seventeen. Angie was cute, and I looked like a nine-year-old. If it wasn't for those three taking me out, the only club I would have been able to get into would have been Sam's Club. (Okay, Sam's wasn't around back then, but you get my point.) Yosepha was our siren. Men were unable to resist her call. As we were leaving a club one night, a pro basketball player spotted Yosepha. Like every man she attracted to our group, he completely forgot that statutory rape came with a jail sentence.

"Ladies, there's a party," he said as we were getting into the car. "Follow me."

Now, we were young and dumb so we did things like that. A guy said, "Follow me," and we said, "Why the heck not?" Yosepha began tailing him, we were all excited.

"Oh, a basketball player!"

"Girl, I know!"

Then we got stuck behind a stoplight. We watched as his car pulled away.

"Aww. Shoot, Yosepha. You're losing him!"

A white limo pulled up next to us. A black window rolled down slowly.

"Where y'all going?" a man asked.

The voice was familiar, but I couldn't quite place him. Then he stuck part of his face out the window and that was all I needed. This man, who was asking us high school seniors where "we all" were going, was a *major* movie star whose name I will take to my grave.

"Oh, we were going to a party, but we got lost," said Yosepha. She was our man-bait, and boy, was she working tonight.

We weren't lost at all, and we could see the basketball player's car in the distance, but who cared about some old NBA guy when a *major* movie star whose name I will take to my grave was flirting with us?

"Well," he said, "me and my friends, we're going somewhere. Why don't you come with us?"

"Sure!" we chimed.

And we followed his limo to a hotel, on Sunset Boulevard in Hollywood. We went up to his suite, and we started talking. Hanging. Laughing, with one of the most famous people on earth. It was surreal. Two of his friends kept going to the bathroom. I was so naive that I asked the *major* movie star whose name I will take to my grave:

"What's up with your friends? They got bladder problems?"

"Oh, they're photographers," he said, with a straight face. "They're developing film."

We believed him.

The four of us look back at that night, and we're astonished at how lucky we were. *Major* movie star could have given us drugs, raped us, and chopped our bodies into little pieces. Instead, nothing happened. We stayed until about 6 AM, talking and laughing while his friends developed film. *Major* movie star whose name I will take to my grave must have realized how young and dumb we were, because he backed off.

I got home at 7 AM. This time, Mom was wide awake and furious.

"WHERE HAVE YOU BEEN?"

"They came home late!" I said, hoping my babysitter lie would work one last night.

"Why didn't you call?"

"The phone was disconnected!"

"How come everyone you sit for has a disconnected phone?"

"The recession," I said, hoping I was using the right word.

"Recession?! How do they contact you about babysitting when they ain't got a phone? What do they use—a carrier pigeon?"

Crap, Mom's mother-detective instincts were kicking in.

"And how come all your families can afford a babysitter, but not a telephone? Who's going out on dates when they can't afford to pay the phone bill?"

I panicked and fell back on my old standby.

"I don't know but I hate you and I can't wait till I'm eighteen so I can move out!"

And I headed out the door for school.

Making up in the nick of time

My poor Mom. I imagine she's in Heaven right now, whispering ideas into Jeffrey's young ears. Because I definitely deserve some payback.

Mom and I became close again shortly before she passed away. As she got sicker, the only thing that helped her fall asleep was taking a drive in the car. She was like a baby that way. I'd go to her house in San Bernardino after work and drive her around for a few hours. Then I'd put her to bed. I was grateful to be able to give back to her, after taking so much.

> *Write yourself a permission slip to call*
> *your mom and tell her how you snuck out*
> *of the house. Even though she probably*
> *already figured it out.*

Daddy's girl

Actually, I'm more than a Daddy's girl. I'm my dad in a wig.

The most satisfying part of my career is being able to share it with my dad. He wanted to be in show business—that was his deferred dream. We have pictures of him on the base in Okinawa, doing stand-up comedy for his fellow troops. Not one picture of him in uniform holding a gun. When Jeffrey asks if his grampa served his country, I'll say, "Of course." And then show him a picture of Dad getting laughs at the officers' club, like George Wallace. (The comedian, of course, not the segregationist governor from Alabama.)

My dad is very involved in my career, and I love it. People always complain about stage mothers living through their kids; well, I'm a "stage child." I *want* my dad to live his dreams through me. That's half the fun, hanging out with, as he calls himself, "Sherri Shepherd's Dad."

When I visit Dad in Chicago, he takes me straight from the airport to people's homes for autographs. I like to tease him.

"Daddy, can we stop off at home so I can take a shower first?"

"No time, Sherri," he'll say, tapping his watch. "No time. We gotta meet Ms. Johnson across the street, Mrs. Hawkins, whose son manages the deli I like, then I got you penciled in at the credit union at 2 PM. I gotta introduce you to Gregory Brown, who handles my account. And there's four new cashiers at the grocery store, and the fruit guy is bringing his mama. Baby, I hope you brought enough headshots. And I got my Sharpie pen, if you need me to sign any of them."

Dad signs my headshots, "All the best, Larry Shepherd. (Sherri Shepherd's Dad.)" Those headshots are more valuable than the ones I sign, so if you come across one on eBay, snatch it up.

Woe to anyone in Chicago who doesn't recognize me. Dad takes this as a personal insult. The last time I was home, we stopped by a White Castle (I only had a Diet Coke, I swear). Well, the manager didn't recognize me and Dad spent about six minutes giving him a rundown on my career.

He would do the same thing before I was famous, too. After I appeared on a little-watched TV show, he took me to the local Jewel and started talking to other shoppers.

"This is my daughter, Sherri. She was on *Totally Hidden Video*. Did you see it?"

"No, I don't think I did."

"Well, I have it on a VHS tape. If you have a VCR, I can send you a copy." Then he'd try to get their addresses.

My dad has a copy of everything I've ever done, on every kind of media. He's got DVDs, VHS tapes, cassette tapes, and probably a cave drawing of me onstage. If I ever get famous enough to merit my own museum, all you'd have to do is hire a tour guide to work Dad's living room, because my entire career is stacked in the corner.

When *Beauty Shop* opened, I took Dad to the premiere. We walked down the red carpet together, and he did an interview with *Access Hollywood*. I just stood to the side and enjoyed watching as he took his moment in the limelight.

> *Write yourself a slip to let somebody brag about you, even if it makes you feel ridiculous. 'Cause it ain't always about you, selfish.*

Dad's awful advice

The only time I have to rein in my dad is when he gives me advice about Hollywood. For many years, he thought that because he managed three McDonald's franchises, he could manage my career.

"Sherri, the people in Hollywood need to know you can do more than one thing. When I hire a young person to work at my restaurant, I need to know they can work the cash register *and* the fry machine."

"Dad, I don't need to work a fry machine to get booked on *Friends.*"

"If you tell them you can also cook, won't that help you?"

"No, Dad."

"Sure it will! If they know you can act, be an extra, *and* help out with lunch, how could they not hire you? Next time you audition, show them you are indispensable. Let those big shots know that you are a triple threat."

Okay. I love my Dad, but I can't imagine auditioning for a director and, as I'm leaving, turning around to say, "You know, I can also help with those sandwiches."

I can always tell when Dad's about to give me advice. He'll say something like, "You know your daddy doesn't want to give you advice."

That's my cue to prepare myself. Because Dad gives what I call "opposite-advice." Whatever advice he gives, I do the exact opposite. It's worked so far.

For instance, when I was working on *Everybody Loves Raymond,* Dad called me, very concerned.

"Sherri, you know I hate to meddle—"

"Uh-oh."

"But you need to get a letter of recommendation from Mr. Romano."

"Dad, that's not how it works here."

"Of course it is. After you finish your performance, you approach Mr. Romano and you say, 'I hope you liked my work.' He's gonna say yes, 'cause you my baby and my baby always does a great job. Then you say, 'Can I get a reference letter?' Now, he's gonna say yes, 'cause nobody says no to Larry Shepherd's baby. Then you make copies of that letter, staple them to the back of every headshot you send out—"

"Dad, seriously, that's not how they do this."

"—and voilà! Sherri, you'll be turning work down. Trust your old man on this."

My dad has given "opposite-advice" to my co-stars.

One of my first sitcoms was a series called *Rewind,* with Scott Baio. I invited Dad to a few live tapings. He sat in the VIP area of the audience.

"Dad," I told him, "please don't say anything that will embarrass me."

I think he heard *do* instead of *don't.* Because a few minutes later, I was talking to Scott and a very familiar voice boomed from the audience.

"Excuse me, Chachi?"

I turned around, Scott turned around. It was Dad, calling Scott Baio the name of his character from *Happy Days*.

"Dad! Shh!" I was mortified. My career was going to end right here, right now, on that soundstage.

"It's okay," Scott said. "My dad does that, too."

"Your dad calls you Chachi?" I asked.

"Chachi," continued Dad, "I think you should give my daughter more lines."

I wanted to die. This was a hundred times worse then selling giraffe paintings next to my high school. But Scott Baio, whom I will love forever, squinted into the stands and said, "You know what, Mr. Shepherd, we just might do that."

Dad was happy, and the rest of the taping went without incident. After he returned to Chicago, my character got *less* lines. But that only convinced him that he should be on the set, all the time.

"Sherri, if you want me to move out there and be your agent," he said, "I will."

I did not take him up on his offer, and he still thinks I made a mistake.

> *Write yourself a permission slip to love your dad, not hire him. This goes double for Jessica Simpson.*

Dad still sells things

My dad is in his sixties and he's still selling stuff. He can't help himself. He's addicted to the multilevel pyramid marketing idea. About every three months, I get a voice mail like this:

"Call your daddy, I got a great new thing going on."

When I return the call, he gives me orders.

"Write down seven people that your daddy can talk to."

The goal of multilevel marketing is to get people working for you. Everyone knocks this as a "pyramid" scheme, but to me, that's the way the world works. The CEO of McDonald's doesn't pop in to a Mickey D's and prepare your Happy Meal. The people under him do it, and he takes home the big bucks. My dad's no different from anyone else who would rather be the CEO. And I'm pretty sure that if I gave him Whoopi Goldberg's phone number, in less than five minutes he would have her working for him.

He's good.

Once he was selling dried fruits and vegetables, in a can. Now, why anyone would allow canned, dried vegetables to enter his digestive system is a question I can't answer, but apparently people do.

"Sherri," he said, "they're so dang healthy!"

"Uh-huh."

"Now, don't you think your Hollywood friends would like to be healthy?"

"Oh no, Daddy," I said. I knew where this was going.

"Why don't you call Ray Romano—"

"Daddy, I ain't calling Ray Romano to sell him no canned vegetables."

"That's fine. Give me his number and I'll call him myself."

"Absolutely not."

"Well, how about I give you a few cans to take to the set. Next time someone says they're hungry, you can pop open a can of corn—"

"Dad!"

"Corn is good for your toenails, you're telling me that Hollywood stars don't care about how their feet look?"

I can't remember how I talked my dad out of sending boxes of canned food to the set. All I know is that somewhere in storage, I have about a year's worth of dried green beans. So if you're reading this and you have a hankering . . . leave me a message on Facebook. I'll get 'em to you.

And don't be shy if you need a lawyer, 'cause guess who's got a connection?

Dad's latest "greatest thing since sliced bread" (or canned apples) is prepaid legal aid. You pay $19.99 a month, and if you ever find yourself in need of a lawyer, well . . . I'll let my dad tell you all about it:

"You can say good-bye to high-priced attorneys that never answer the phone, because these guys pick up the phone twenty-four hours a day. And you can upgrade, anytime, to $49.99 a month. It's still a bargain."

I bought the low-end version, just in case. The upgrade was out of my price range.

Dad watches me on *The View* every day. Now, I do feel bad for my loved ones. Because I do not have a filter. If a thought pops in my head, scoot over, because it's comin' out my mouth. It happens that fast, and sometimes I don't realize I've stepped over the Shepherd Family Line until it's too late. I'll get home and see that I got a bunch of texts from my dad.

"Call ur daddy"

"what do u mean when u said u slept with a lot of men?"

"??????????????"

"how many is a lot?"

"no dont tell me"

"!!!!!!!!!!!!!!"

The downside of being "Sherri Shepherd's Daddy" is that Sherri Shepherd sometimes does dumb things.

Like this next story . . .

The photo album lesson

Dad is remarried, and he has been a church deacon for a long time. Shortly after I found Christ, Dad and his new wife, also a Christian, came to visit me. I guess he wanted to show off his old baby to his new one. He pulled out a photo album and started flipping through it, proudly. I could hear them from the kitchen. I had a bad feeling in my gut, but I couldn't figure out why.

"Look at this here," my dad said, his voice booming, "Sherri's about five years old here. Now, this little girl had the love of the Lord all over her. She knew her Bible verses from Genesis to Revelation. A true child of God, my girl Sherri."

I heard his new wife say, "So precious." Another chill down my spine, but again, I didn't know why.

"And this is my Sherri, about eleven years old," Dad continued. "She sang in the junior choir, knew the words to 'Yes Jesus Loves Me,' 'This Little Light of Mine.' Just a pleasure."

I heard his new wife say, "So sweet." Then that fuzzy feeling became clear. *Oh my God.* I had posed semi- and completely naked for an ex-boyfriend. And I stuck the photos—NO!

"Dad," I shouted, trying to stop time. "Don't turn that page!"

I ran from the kitchen, but I was a split second too late.

"And this is," Dad was saying. "Oh my heavens."

He slammed the book shut. His new wife didn't say anything.

"Daddy, I'm so sorry. Those photos were taken before Jesus came into my life. I keep them because I happened to look great even though I was in a spiritual crisis."

And Dad, for the first time in my life, remained silent.

We are family

We're very close, my sisters and I. Lauren, the baby, is hyper-responsible. She's a perfectionist, like our mom. Lauren likes her ducks lined up, in rows and quacking to the beat. Her daughter is so well behaved, it's scary. Lauren will not hesitate to give her opinion. In fact, both my little sisters are bossy, and they like to practice on me.

After I had Jeffrey, I decided I would not be whuppin' him. I told Lauren, "I'm not gonna spank my son. I'm gonna talk to him."

"Oh, please," she said, rolling her eyes. "You've been hanging out with too many white people. Quit that mess, pop his behind and he will know you mean business."

"Dang! Can I get him out of intensive care first?!" After all, my son did spend the first months of his life in the neonatal intensive care unit.

"Don't be weak," she said, shaking her head.

"You ain't been whupped but once, why are you telling me how to do it?"

When Lauren came to visit us in New York, Jeffrey's hair was out, in total 'fro mode. She almost kidnapped him.

"You need to cut that Afro," she said.

"Aw, it's cute."

"Give me that child." She scooped Jeffrey up like she was

going to put him in her suitcase. "Give him to me for three weeks. I will have him in shape. He will be yes-ma'am-ing and no-ma'am-ing. His hair will be short and respectable. He'll have a job before he's five."

I haven't done that yet, but it's nice to know I got a family-run boot camp, ready to enlist my son should he start acting up.

I admire both my sisters so much. Lisa's had some tough times, and being a middle child didn't help. The oldest and the baby always get so much attention. The middles seem to get lost in the mix. Well, Lisa is a mother to five children now and she just put herself through school so she could be a nursing assistant. Of course, she still finds the time to call and get on me about things I say on *The View*.

"Why didn't you say *this* when you were sitting at the table when so-and-so said *that!* Why didn't you?"

I never have a good answer. And there are days I would like to channel Lisa's mouth and really own that table. Because if she'll tell a bunch of Jehovah's Witnesses to pick up their Bibles and hit the bricks, she will not back down during Hot Topics.

All in all, a lucky lady

Grateful is how I'd describe myself when it comes to my family. My dad is still alive and as long as I keep ignoring his advice, we'll continue to be best friends. My sisters are strong women who do not back down. When I'm feeling nonconfrontational on *The View*, I pretend to be Lisa or Lauren, and then I get my point across. I was lucky enough to make peace with my mom before she passed on. Some of my female friends aren't there yet, and their mothers are well into their seventies.

I learned from the things they did right, and the things they did wrong. And now I'm looking forward to making a whole new set of mistakes on my own son.

> *So write yourself a permission slip to love the parts of your family that are lovable, and forgive the rest.*

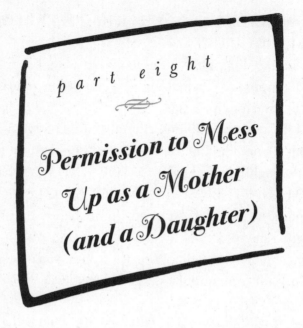

Permission to Mess Up as a Mother (and a Daughter)

Once I read a news story about a reunion between two Vietnam War vets. One was American, the other Vietnamese. Decades after fighting each other, they were able to meet and reminisce. The former enemies now respected each other as warriors and survivors. I like that story a lot because it reminds me of how my dad and I talk about my childhood. Like a couple of war vets looking back on a mighty battle.

I took my dad to Orlando. I was hosting an event and he was being Sherri Shepherd's Dad.

"Dad, I need to apologize for how much of a jerk I was growing up. I want you to know how much I appreciate you."

"Aww, I forgive you," he said. "Remember when you almost ran away? You'd just started saying that thing that made your mother and me want to turn you over to the foster care system," he said.

He started to mimic me, rolling his neck. "I HATE—"

I jumped in.

"—YOU AND I CAN'T WAIT TILL I'M EIGHTEEN SO I CAN MOVE OUT!"

Ah yes, like singing the lyrics to an old song. I should trademark that phrase so I can make money every time some backtalking brat like me uses it.

Yes, I did remember almost running away. I forget why I was angry, but it's not like I needed a good reason. I was a teenager, that was enough. I hurled I HATE YOU AND I CAN'T WAIT TILL I'M EIGHTEEN SO I CAN MOVE OUT™ at my dad, and prepared to stomp dramatically to my bedroom. Oh, how I loved a good stomp.

"Eighteen?" Dad said. "Why wait until you're eighteen— that's four years from now. Hey, I got a great idea. Why don't you move out now?"

"Fine!" I said, shocked that *I* was agreeing. "I'd be happy to!"

And there we were, two Shepherds, staring each other down in the kitchen. If this had been a spaghetti western, that Clint Eastwood whistle would have played.

"I don't need you. I'm outta here," I said. I stomped to my bedroom and started throwing things in a suitcase. I already knew where I was going—Mrs. Ramsey's house.

Monica Ramsey's mom was the coolest mom on the block. You could talk to her about anything and stay over late, until eight o'clock. I knew Mrs. Ramsey would be thrilled to take me in.

"Oh no," said my dad. He was standing in my doorway. "This suitcase belongs to me." He emptied its contents on the floor.

"Fine," I said. I decided to act as if this had been part of my plan all along. "I got arms, I'll just carry things."

"What things?" he asked.

"My phone," I said, grabbing my Mickey Mouse phone.

"*Whose* phone? That's my phone. Give it here." Dad took Mickey out of my hands.

"Fine," I said, reaching in the closet for my Michael Jackson jacket.

"That's your sister's now," he said.

"You gonna give Lisa my Michael Jackson jacket?"

"I'll give *my* jacket to whoever I want. Leave it on the hanger."

Lisa in my jacket? This was bordering on disrespectful. I reached for my Holly Hobby quilt.

"Mine," said Dad.

"Dad, you ain't gonna sleep under a Holly Hobby quilt!"

"You never know, I like that little gal. Give it here."

I was down to the shirt on my back and the Gloria Vanderbilts on my butt. Shoot. Well, surely Dad wouldn't prevent me from taking some extra undergarments, right?

"And who do you think owns those underpants?"

"I don't even own my *panties*?" I asked, exasperated.

"That's right. Put them back in the drawer. Your mother can give them a wash and send them to Goodwill."

My Monday through Sundays, at a Goodwill? This is not how the kids ran away on *Eight Is Enough*. They took suitcases and the stepmom packed a lunch. I wasn't even getting a red bandanna tied to a stick.

"Sherri, you don't get to take anything from this house. Nothing in this bedroom belongs to you."

"Fine," I said, stomping down the stairs. I would just leave with the clothes I was wearing, and I'd better do it fast before Dad figured out those were his, too.

"And Sherri," Dad said, "when you leave, you can't come back. You cannot come back to this house. So you think about that before you walk out the door."

I slowed my stomp to a trudge. My mom and sisters were crying in the hallway. Wow, everyone seemed to be taking this seriously.

"So get out," Dad called, "you want to be grown, be grown. Get out. Good-bye."

I put my hand on the front door, ready to twist. Ready to move into Mrs. Ramsey's house. With no toothbrush and wearing panties that would be dirty tomorrow.

"I'm going to give you a choice, Sherri," he said. He was right behind me now. "You can walk out that door, or you can stay."

A thousand thoughts went through my head. *What if Mrs. Ramsey doesn't let me stay? Where will I go? How will I get to school? Wait, where is school?*

I took my hand off the knob.

"Dad, I'm choosing to stay." I tried to spin it like I was doing him a favor, but he wasn't having any of it.

"If you choose to stay, do you promise to follow my rules?" Dad asked.

"Fine."

"Then get on upstairs, make up your bed, and come downstairs for dinner."

Shoot. I had blinked. If this had been an old spaghetti western, no one would've got shot, and the audience would've asked for their money back.

Now that we were reminiscing in Orlando, I wanted an answer.

"Dad, were you really gonna kick me out?" I asked.

"Nope. If you had left, I would have begged you to stay."

"Dad, are you freakin' kidding me? If I'd have known that, I would have walked out that door."

"There is no way I would have let my baby leave the house. Thank God you didn't call my bluff."

"How many times did that happen? All that trash-talking— you couldn't even back it up!"

"I can't even count. Once a day. And every time I would pray,

Please, Lord, do not let that girl call my bluff because I have no idea what I'm doing."

So there you go. All those years that I thought my dad knew everything, he was bluffing. I'm actually relieved to hear that. Because at least once a day, I look at Jeffrey and pray, *Please, Lord, do not let that boy call my bluff because I have no idea what I'm doing.*

Like father, like daughter.

Karate kid

The first time I laid eyes on my one-pound son, I thought, *My goodness, if I don't get you to a karate class, you are going to have the crap beat out of you every day for the rest of your life.*

You were probably expecting something more heartfelt. Sorry, I've been a comedian too long. My instincts take over during times of high stress, and this was one of those times.

I had gone into labor the day before. I didn't realize it at first. My pregnancy had been so filled with drama that the contraction just felt like another thing gone wrong. And besides, at twenty-five weeks, I wasn't expecting to deliver my baby for about four more months. In fact, since this would be my last childless birthday, I'd rented a limo and planned a day alone at the beach in Malibu. I wanted to smell salty air, and get some perspective on my husband's affair.

Malibu is about three hours away with traffic. And there's always traffic. Just as the limo was pulling up to my driveway, I felt a second deep and pervasive pain in my abdomen.

Let me tell you about a contraction. It feels like someone left a Hand—capital H—in your stomach, and every few minutes the Hand gathers up every nerve ending in your body and squeezes them as hard as it can, just to be a jerk. And just when you are about to confess America's nuclear secrets to Russia, the Hand lets go.

After the third contraction, I'd had enough. I sent the limo away and called for my husband.

"Jeff, we got to get to the hospital!"

He drove fast. And because this was about the hundredth time during this pregnancy that we were running red lights to get to the ER, I insisted we slow down, stop, and grab a few Big Macs. This was back when I was a "pre." And I would be damned if I was gonna let searing pain get in the way of a good combo meal.

At the hospital, the doctor decided to keep me overnight. Crap. Again. And tomorrow was my birthday. I woke up the next morning, ready to be released. I dangled my legs off the side of the bed, pushed myself to a standing position, and felt a familiar whoosh.

Blood, gushing out of me.

I was more aggravated than panicked, as blood had been whooshing out of me since I'd miscarried my son's twin. Cleaning a puddle off the floor was practically part of my daily routine. The doctors weren't as blasé. They came at me with stethoscopes blazing, just like the doctors on *ER*.

"We're losing the baby's heartbeat. We need to take him now."

"Take him?" I asked.

"Deliver him. We are delivering the baby now."

I was rushed to a delivery room. I felt a warm washcloth on my privates. A nurse was cleaning me, gently, and shaving.

"I'm so sorry you got to see all of this," I said. I was mortified. I hadn't tended to "the garden" in a few days—what was going on down there? I apologized again. "My husband don't even see me like this."

"It's okay," she said. She spoke with a soft German accent. "It's okay."

Lord, I prayed silently, *please let something good happen to this nice lady, because she*—SQUEEZE.

"AAAAAAAAH," I screamed, forgetting all about my prayer. The Hand was back, and this time it was trying to make my eyeballs pop out.

"You want an epidural?" someone asked.

"AAAAAAH!"

"Is that a yes?"

"AAAAAHHHHH-OH-OH-OH-OH-OH."

"Okay, Sherri, push back. Push your back up against the needle."

I guess I did that. I can't remember, the pain was blinding.

"It ain't working!" I said.

And then, all of a sudden, it worked. The Hand unclenched, went limp, and then just walked away, like Thing from the Addams Family. I couldn't feel my legs. I passed out for a few seconds and when I woke up, I was staring into ten mirrored lights. It was like looking up into a giant spider's eye. People in scrubs were bent over me, looking concerned.

I farted. Normally I would have been embarrassed, but childbirth lowers your humiliation standards. I passed out again, and that's when my son was born. I wasn't conscious when they pulled Jeffrey out of me. He'd been without oxygen for two minutes, and according to my husband, his body was limp.

A SWAT team of doctors burst through the door to work on my tiny, limp son. I was still out. My husband thought we were both dead. When I regained consciousness again, I thought the same thing. Bright lights above me, my loved ones surrounding me. *I had a baby and I died? This birthday sucks,* I told God, whom I assumed was nearby, signing off on my final paperwork.

Jeffrey had been taken directly to the NICU, where he would

live in a plastic bubble for three and a half months. My husband and I would not be allowed to hold our newborn for weeks. But for reasons I can't really explain, when I first laid eyes on Jeffrey, I was not shocked by his tiny body, or the breathing machine, or the tubes and IVs.

I was shocked by his hair.

Babies aren't as cute as we think they are

Now, all babies are born goofy looking (yes, even yours—be honest), but Jeffrey's goofy level was off the charts and it was all because of his hair. Or not-hair. Jeffrey's hairline started and ended at the back of his neck. He looked like an Irish monk. So that's why, when I met my son for the first time, I vowed to enroll him in some kind of self-defense class.

Because kids are evil.

Kids will make fun of anything, and if you've got no weak points, they will make up stuff about you so they can make fun of you. They will say your daddy's gay when he's not, that your sister's got six toes on each foot when she doesn't. So for Jeffrey to be showing up for class, handing these kids his giant forehead on a silver platter? Oh boy.

I imagined him in school, walking down the halls, the other kids saying, "How's it going, Forehead?"

And you know how kids are. As soon as they take their first sex education class, they're gonna change Forehead to Foreskin. And he's black, so they'll probably change that to Bro-Skin. And that one's gonna stick. So when he graduates from college and sets up a job interview, a potential employer's gonna go to his Facebook page, look at his wall, and the first question they're gonna ask my baby is, "What's Bro-Skin mean?"

Oh Lord, I prayed, watching Jeffrey through a plastic bubble, *how's he gonna get a job?*

Then I saw, really saw, all the tubes in my baby's little body. Tubes in his nose, down his throat, in his chest. Even tubes in his feet. Breathing on a ventilator, not knowing that this was his mom looking at him behind this sheet of plastic. And I felt like I'd been punched hard in the stomach.

> *So write yourself a permission slip to see the funny part first. Misery is patient, and will wait.*

Don't be brave, take drugs

The best advice I never took came from my friend Niecy Nash, who warned me about the aftermath of my C-section.

"Sherri, bind up your stomach. Take a sheet and wrap it tightly like a girdle. Pull it, because if you don't, you're going to have this flab. But if you pull it now, your stomach's going to be flat as a board."

I have no idea if that's an old wives' tale. All I know is I didn't do it, and I have a shelf of stomach fat that could hold a set of encyclopedias.

The post-op pain was indescribable. Here, let me give it a

shot: Imagine a thousand knives being driven into your abdomen. Hmm. Nope, I just reread that sentence and it doesn't come close. I'll go back to my original theory: C-section pain is indescribable.

I was released after a week, which was, in my estimate, about a month too soon.

You just cut open my belly and pulled a person out of me. Can I just lay here for a few weeks and get my damn bearings, please? What is the rush?

"We need the bed," someone in scrubs told me.

My doctor gave me a prescription for Vicodin, but I decided that I didn't need them. I'd read about too many celebrities who get addicted to "painkillers," whatever that means, and with my family's history, why risk it? I threw the prescription away. Ironically, when I decided to forgo painkillers, I was under the influence of painkillers. (The hospital doped me up pretty good.) It was only after the Vicodin wore off that I realized what a grave mistake I'd made. I crawled on my hands and knees to the kitchen and foraged like a homeless person through my garbage, looking for that little piece of paper.

I couldn't find it.

Niecy came to visit and starting getting on me.

"Sherri, you better wrap up your stomach." She came at me, like she was gonna do it.

"STAY AWAY!" Since pulling the bedsheet over my stomach felt like a murder attempt, I would not be binding it without the presence of an anesthesiologist. "Niecy, you better get out my room because the last thing I'm thinking about is a flat belly."

Believe me, I think about it now. Every time I try on a pair of jeans.

> ***So write yourself a permission slip
> to do hard things the easy way. And if
> you're a doctor, please write me, Sherri
> Shepherd, a permission slip for Vicodin.***

I became that lady I once mocked

Karma is real. I know this because I have become one of those women I used to make fun of. While I recovered from my C-section, I was that patient who walks slow, in fat white socks, while her robe keeps opening in the back, exposing her butt to the sick and dying.

My daily walk to the NICU was like a trek up Kilimanjaro. I was bent over from pain, crippled by gas. Yes, gas. Backed-up farts were bringing this girl to her knees. And no wig. Before childbirth, I wouldn't shower unless one of my wigs was nearby, ready to pop on my head in case of an emergency.

Yet here I was, my behind was showing and visitors were laughing. I knew it was me they were laughing at because I laughed that same laugh during my callous youth while visiting my family in the hospital. Here I was, finally getting served, and I didn't have enough sass in my frass to say something back.

I did not care.

Dignity? Gone. I needed assistance getting off the toilet. And forget wiping myself. A nurse had to spray water on my privates and wipe *for* me. One night, I apologized to the Filipino nurse who was taking care of me.

"I'm so sorry you got to do this."

"It's my job," she said. "I don't mind."

Then she helped me into bed.

There's a special place in Heaven for nurses, and I hope it's a place where everyone can wipe their own bottom.

Fairy tales don't come true

It's hard to cradle a newborn when you're not allowed to touch him. When they brought me to Jeffrey, I wanted to rub his arms and let him know that Mom was there.

"No, you can't do that 'cause he's got sensory issues," said the nurse. "You think you're touching his arm lightly, but to him it feels like sandpaper on his skin."

"So you're telling me that my touch is irritating?"

"Basically."

I was frustrated because the one thing I had to offer, he didn't want. I'm not ashamed to say that it took me a little while to bond with my son, and let's be honest, Jeffrey wasn't helping. His eyes stayed closed for two months. Even if they fluttered open, they would close quickly. He never looked at me. I wasn't getting that mother–child thing you see on the pregnancy shows on TLC.

It was tough seeing the other moms holding their newborns, and passing them around to family members. I was jealous of how easy they had it. Sometimes when I visited Jeffrey, I felt like I was behind the food counter at a deli, and I had to take a number and ask the nurse to give me one pound of my son, please.

Jeffrey also had this nasty habit of almost dying. His heart would stop, machines would sound, a team of doctors would rush in and ask me to get out of the way.

"Wake up, Jeffrey," I remember a nurse shouting, tapping on his feet. "Wake up!"

This happened all the time. From the moment he was born, it was clear he could die at any time. There was a hole in his heart, and his intestine. His lungs were underdeveloped. Heck, everything was underdeveloped because he was supposed to cook in my oven for four more months.

I was detached. I think I had to be, or else I would've been crushed by despair.

My comeback kid

"Your son has Grade 4 brain bleeding, which is the worst. He will probably need shunts in his brain for the rest of his life," a doctor said.

I was so numb that I couldn't even pray. I was unable to say God's name or ask Him for help, because I couldn't even form sentences. Words were beyond me. All I could do was repeat, in my head, some scripture I'd read a thousand times, Jeremiah 1:5. *Before I formed you in the belly I knew you.*

"The odds of your son having cerebral palsy are very high. He may never be able to move the left side of his body. He may suffer severe retardation."

And before you came forth out of the womb I sanctified you.

"His stomach is that color because he has a hole in his intestine, which is causing a dangerous infection."

And I ordained you a prophet to the nations.

For the second time in my life, I was going to pull the plug on a ventilator, so someone I loved could go home to God. I was in shock. The doctors predicted that if Jeffrey lived, his life would be one of pain and surgeries. I feared that keeping him alive, because I wanted a baby, was selfish. And if God wanted him back that badly, well, I would have to make peace with that.

I knew Jeffrey would be met first in Heaven by his twin sister, and then his grandmother and his uncles and so many souls who loved him. No tubes, no pain, just love. And that I could see him when it was my turn.

My husband and I prepared to let our son go. A social worker helped us pick out an urn. We bought a very tiny outfit, and a teddy bear. A few girlfriends, who'd been praying with me for weeks, came to the hospital. We prayed again, hoping we could comfort this motionless little body before us.

Jeff, my husband, lifted the dome off the isolette. The baby lay there as he had every day before, slowly inhaling and exhaling.

"Son," my husband said, "your mom's here. Say hi."

Jeffrey's right hand came up, and then it came back down. A thousand chills shot up my spine. He had never moved on his own before. Then Jeffrey took his right hand and gripped his ventilator tube so hard that his knuckles turned white. In retrospect, it was like he was saying, "I hear y'all praying and wailing, and I would just like you to know that I'm still using this thing so please don't turn it off!"

I fell further into agony. We were going ahead with the disconnection because of his prognosis, but after what I'd just seen, something didn't feel right. Or, it did feel right, for the first time since his birth.

Now I was holding my son. Our plan was to let him take his last breath in my arms. I could make the call at any time, but I was paralyzed. These moments, with my son cradled in my arms, were all I'd craved since he was born, and I wanted each one. They were mine. Then, slowly, I began to feel like I couldn't keep taking from Jeffrey. It was his time to go. I said the Lord's Prayer out loud.

Deep breath. Okay.

The chief of the NICU walked into our room.

"Mrs. Shepherd, we did another ultrasound and the hole in Jeffrey's intestine is healed. There's no hole. It's fine."

I screamed. We all screamed. After losing every battle so far, our little Jeffrey had finally won a battle. A major battle.

"Sometimes it happens," the doctor continued. "Sometimes things heal themselves. We've seen crazy things happen."

I guess doctors have a policy against calling something a miracle. I don't. I heard God say, "Sherri, you don't get to decide when this baby comes home. I do."

"We're not taking him off this ventilator," my husband said.

That decision was not popular. The woman who was helping us pick out urns gave us a host of grim statistics.

"We studied sixty babies born at twenty-five weeks, and the odds of mental retardation and cerebral palsy are—"

"I'm sorry," I said, "but sixty babies ain't enough. You need to study six thousand babies before you tell me to let my son go."

My husband was of the same mind. "If our son is going to fight, then we're going to fight," he said.

Later, Jeff told me that when he prayed, he told God that he'd take whatever he could get. "Lord, if You just bless my baby to stay alive, whatever package he comes in, I'll accept and be as happy as I could be. If he's in a wheelchair, I'll take him in a wheelchair to the football game. I don't care how he comes wrapped. I accept the package."

And the miracles kept coming. Jeffrey's belly turned from black and blue to a beautiful chocolate brown. The bleeding in his brain stopped. Doctors are funny about how they inform you of incredibly good news. They don't jump up and down or hug you. It's like they're telling you about a parking ticket.

"The blood in your son's brain resolved itself," the doctor told me. "There's no more bleeding, so he won't have to have the shunts."

"It's a miracle!" I shrieked.

"Well, you know. It happens."

"*It happens*," I said, making fun of him. "Hey, I'm going with 'It's a miracle.' How about that?"

He shrugged, and probably went off to tell someone else that their cancer was terminal. I guess doctors can't get emotionally invested in either outcome.

Time heals

I would visit Jeffrey in the NICU three or four times a day. Willing that little guy into good health became my sole reason for living. Despite our miracles, I was very depressed. I couldn't imagine doing comedy ever again.

"I don't have it in me to make people laugh and I don't care about anything," I told my dad. "I won't ever be able to get onto a stage, 'cause my baby is fighting for his life. What do I have to laugh about?"

"Time heals wounds, Sherri, it's true," Dad said, "Jeffrey will come home and you will forget some of this pain."

He was right. My memories of the NICU come in small doses. Tiny flashes. Some moments hit me even now and I can't breathe. When Jeffrey got to be three pounds, we started doing something called "Kangaroo Care." It's basically skin-on-skin contact, and it helps the babies heal faster. Jeffrey was lying on my chest, and we were both so happy and comfortable, we fell asleep.

One time, Jeffrey's heart stopped. That would happen when he went into a deep sleep. I was awakened by nurses grabbing my son off my body, shouting, "He's flatlining. Jeffrey, wake up! Jeffrey, wake up!"

I began crying, "Oh my gosh, not again!"

"Mrs. Shepherd, you have to go," said a nurse. "We got to get this together."

And I was led out of the room, as grown-ups thumped and tapped on my three-pound baby's body, bringing him back to life again.

> *So write yourself a permission slip to forget a few bad memories. Write 'em down first, for the grandkids, and then let them go. Nobody will notice, and you'll sleep better tonight.*

Doing the only thing I could do

When you produce milk, it is exactly what your baby needs at that time. Even when they're born premature. So there was *one* thing that only I could do for Jeffrey: pump milk.

That's exactly what I did. Every two hours, for three months, I pumped a batch of milk. And it would take me about forty minutes to fill half a bottle. Because it wasn't like I'd wake, squirt, and fall asleep. No, that would be too easy for Sherri Shepherd. For some reason, my breasts, which I believe we have established are *freaking huge*, nonetheless produce very little milk.

That was the icing on the cake. I could accept Jeffrey's condition, and pray for the strength to deal with it, but when my boobs failed me, I told God that I wasn't speaking to Him for about an hour. I was that pissed. In fact, having a pair of useless breasts was more than disappointing, it was insulting. I'd endured years of catcalls and back pain, thinking it would all pay off when I could feed my baby in five seconds flat. And it turns out I can't do that right.

Even worse, a couple of the flat-chested moms in NICU could've stuck taps on their nipples and opened a baby bar.

So every two hours, I would will each drop out of my breast, save it in the fridge, and about an hour and fifteen minutes later do it again. That damn pump and I were attached at the tit. I pumped at Bible study, I pumped at auditions. Once, the receptionist told me to pump in the "executive room" because no one was using it that day. Naturally, as soon as I had everything out, a bunch of executives tried to come in for a meeting.

"Mother in here pumping! Mother pumping!" I shouted, blocking the door with my foot.

They postponed.

Every day, I'd take my bottles to the hospital, and the milk would be delivered to Jeffrey via syringe or IV. One night, I left the freezer door ajar, and the next morning I found a day's worth of bottles that had to be thrown away. I sat in the middle of the kitchen floor and sobbed. My husband was as helpful as most men are in these situations.

"Sherri, what are you crying for?" he asked. I could tell from the tone of his voice that I made no sense to him, at all.

"My milk thawed," I said, demoralized.

"Well, you can always pump more."

I was too tired to kill him, so I just yelled.

"YOU DON'T UNDERSTAND! THIS IS JEFFREY'S

LIFE FORCE AND I CAN'T AFFORD TO LOSE A SINGLE DROP!"

He didn't reply. I could tell he was thinking, *What's the big deal, just pump more.* Often I would ask him to sit with me while I pumped at night, and on the rare occasions he said yes, he'd still fall asleep.

Oh, sleep. I miss you more than I've ever missed any man in my life.

I'll sleep when I'm dead . . . somebody kill me

Many times during Jeffrey's first year, I thought the change in life-style would kill me. If there's one thing that comedians get enough of, it's sleep. Infants and comedians average about sixteen hours of sleep per day. (Working thirty minutes a night is exhausting.) To me, ten hours of sleep is a civil right that should be guaranteed in the Constitution if it is not already. In fact, I'll put it on a par with free speech, because if you're overtired, nothing you say is gonna make sense anyway.

Well, Jeffrey's three now, and I'm still not caught up.

Forcing my agent to look at my nipple

Toward the end of Jeffrey's hospital stay, I was allowed to breast-feed. I'd always been one of those people who pooh-poohed breast-feeders; I thought they were a bunch of hippies and I liked to point out that plenty of presidents were formula-fed. (Which ones, I don't know, but no one ever argued against me.)

But the first time Jeffrey put his lips around my nipple and I got that suck? *Oh wow.* I finally felt like his mother. Because nobody could do that but me. Finally, after all the doctors and all the IVs and surgeries, finally my boy had to depend on me. It felt great. That's when we bonded. I was so excited, I invited everyone I knew to come watch. And when my agents showed up, I couldn't pull my boobs out fast enough.

"You gotta see this! This is a miracle right here. Only a woman can do this. Watch me take this titty and put it in this baby's mouth!"

> *So write yourself a slip to celebrate whatever victories you get, and if you have to pull out a boob to do it, no one will mind.*

Bringing him home

Mr. Miracle came home in August. On release day, my husband and I were given a lesson on how to work an oxygen tank and a heart monitor.

"This is too much. Can't he stay here?" I asked. "You guys are doing a great job, I'm probably gonna turn a knob the wrong way and kill him."

"He's ready to go home, Mrs. Shepherd," the doctor said.

"No he's not!" Jeffrey only weighed four pounds. I was afraid the hospital was sending him home for the same reason they sent me home—they needed the bed. Plus he had a hernia, in his testicle. I felt completely unqualified to deal with my son's balls. It was too much.

For the first two weeks, he screamed all night long. My husband had booked a commercial, so he was gone. I was alone and I could not comfort my son. I'm sure most moms feel this way, but I didn't know if the problem was me, or him, or just the simple fact that he was a baby and that's what babies do.

I don't want this baby, God, I prayed, rocking him, *I don't want him. I can't make him quit!*

While Jeffrey's cries always woke me up, they had an opposite effect on my husband.

"WAAAAAAAAAAAA."

"Jeff, I'm so tired. Can you take him this time?"

"Yeah, give me twenty minutes."

I swear a baby's cry can put a man to sleep faster than Ambien. I'd take Jeffrey for a while, and then try again.

"Okay, it's been twenty minutes. Please take care of your son."

"Sherri, put him down, he's fine."

"What do you mean he's fine?"

"He's fine. Put the baby in his crib, and don't be wearing any clothes when you come back to bed."

Getting used to my new life

Even with all my prayers and fancy talk in the hospital, after I came home with my baby, I was deeply disappointed in motherhood.

I kept comparing my reality with the movies. Giggling babies, sleeping babies, changing diapers. I had a crying baby who kept pulling the tubes out of his nose. His skin was blistered from the heart monitor, and every time I had to pull off tape, he screamed in agony. He was too young to have the hernia removed, so again, his only solution was to cry.

That first week, I looked at my son and thought, *I don't want you. You're broken.*

But soon I found my sea legs. I understood what his cries meant, I became a pro with the equipment. I think it takes time for any new mother to be confident in her abilities, and it took me a little bit longer.

I realized that I resented my husband. Beyond the affair, which we were just starting to deal with, was the child-care issue. We were supposed to be sharing this responsibility, and we weren't, not by a long shot. I was doing most of the grunt work, and during Jeffrey's first weeks home I realized it would always be that way.

After I transferred my anger over to my husband where I realized it belonged, things started to fall into place.

Sometimes, experts are wrong

My son never developed cerebral palsy, and he has no mental retardation. His left side is weaker, but we work with a physical therapist. He is not even slightly paralyzed.

At one point, I had to stop taking him to the neurologist. They wanted to keep tabs on him, to check for CP. So Jeffrey would be at the appointment, playing with blocks.

"Look," I'd say, "he's engaged, he's playing."

"Well, Mrs. Shepherd, we still don't know."

CP affects muscle control, so all babies look like they have it, especially to a nervous mother. Same thing with autism—I was on the Internet constantly, looking for things to look for.

"Does your baby walk on his tiptoes?"

"Yes."

"Does he flap his arms?"

"Yes."

"Is he a boy?"

"OHMYGODMYBABYGOTAUTISM!"

One day, I looked Jeffrey in the eye and made him a promise.

"I'm gonna let this go, because I'm going to drive myself out of this world. And I just got to accept and love you for who you are. And not compare you with anybody else. Okay?"

"Baaaaaaaaf," he said.

And that was good enough for me.

After I decided to let it go, a therapist examined him. I asked when she thought he'd be cleared for cerebral palsy or retardation.

"Oh my, Mrs. Shepherd, your son doesn't have CP."

I started crying with relief.

"What about retardation? They said maybe severe retardation."

"No, no, no. He's slower to learn, yes. He's got disabilities, but he's fine. And he's picking up stuff like crazy."

And that's been the way it's gone. My son does everything, just a little later than yours. When the pediatrician says Jeffrey's in a lower percentile, I let it go. That's doctor-talk. He almost died, now *that's* a low percentile. Anything above ground is 100 percentile to me. I'm grateful that my son runs across the floor, across the room—that he can run at all.

When we meet kids who are speaking in complete sentences, and Jeffrey is responding in gibberish, I think, *That's okay, son, you go at your own pace.* I'm enjoying who he is and what he does right now. Besides, my son has one four-word sentence down pat.

"Mama, I love you."

Every picture tells a (old) story

Jeffrey grew into a typical toddler and oddly enough, that was very difficult for me. All those hospital code blues had left me a wreck, and by his third birthday I had grown very overprotective of his physical health. I, too, had a four-word sentence down pat: "No no, Jeffrey, DON'T!"

My boy is a *boy*. He likes to jump and bump, he likes to throw balls, kick walls, run fast, and hit hard. But for a long time, I couldn't see him as anything but a dying preemie with tubes up his nose. And so I was always yelling at him. *Get down, get up, put that down, pick that up.* It was all negative, all "no." Me and my little man, we weren't having any fun.

My friend Rhonda from Chicago helped me snap out of it.

I had hung photos from Jeffrey's first few months all over my house. Jeffrey at one pound, Jeffrey fitting in the nurse's hand, Jeffrey in the isolation tent, Jeffrey hooked up to an oxygen machine, Jeffrey with an IV. Everywhere I looked, on every wall, was a graphic montage of my fragile, nearly broken baby.

Rhonda, if you recall, became a mom at fourteen. After seeing me interact with Jeffrey at the park, she sat me down and told me I was harming my son.

"Sherri, he's got to start stepping outside of his comfort zone. Let him climb the monkey bars and fall, because that's the only way he'll learn how to get up. You're not letting him learn how to bounce back. He's fine, yet you keep seeing him as this little disabled boy." She pointed to all my photos. "You have to put those away, because that's not who your son is anymore."

That was pretty painful to hear. Jeffrey had so much going against him, I didn't want to be another obstacle that he would have to overcome.

"You don't understand," I said, "he's been through so much. I don't want him to ever spend another day in the hospital."

"I do understand, but you have to see your son as a normal little boy because right now, you are holding him back."

I looked at Jeffrey. He was big now, normal-size. Skinny legs but a nice, fat tummy. Healthy, noisy, alive.

He lived.

I guess it hit me right then, how worried I'd been for so long. For years now, actually. Trying to get pregnant with one, getting pregnant with two, losing the girl, almost losing the boy. Waking up in my own blood, nearly every day, wondering if my boy was mixed up in all that mess. Giving birth during my fifth month. How tiny he was, and how lifeless he seemed until I let him go, until I told God, *Okay, he's Yours,* and somehow Jeffrey heard me and said, *No, Mama, I'm yours.* And how he grabbed the ventilator with his ferocious little doll hand and held on until the doctor pronounced him alive.

I broke down. Cried hard. Cried one of those cries that comes from the center of your body and shreds your insides. I cried until I was done. Dusted myself off. My son is alive. He likes to climb and jump and run, and that's okay.

Help, I've fallen and my mom won't help me up!

Giving up the baby-talk was hard, but in general, this laid-back style of parenting fits in with my natural desire to sit on a bench and watch. Getting up every ten seconds and checking for scratches is for the birds. Now if my son falls, I shout, "Jeffrey, you gonna live? Yes? All right, then get up and try it again."

Once I was putting on makeup, and Jeffrey was jumping on my bed. I could see him in the mirror.

"Sit down," I said, working some eyeliner. "If you don't sit down, I'm not responsible."

He laughed and jumped. In the mirror, I saw him go up. And then . . . he was gone. I did not see him come down. Apparently he slid off the bed. He bit his lip, and blood was gushing. It was one of those times where you remember how you used to be. The old me woulda been halfway to the hospital, pushing old ladies out of my path, "Get outta my way, he was a preemie!"

The new me was like, "Well, I hope you learned to listen to your mom."

Rhonda helped me put up new photographs. Jeffrey running, Jeffrey jumping, Jeffrey hollering. Those photos helped Jeffrey see himself differently, too. He was three years old and still sucking on a binky. I wasn't having any luck getting him to let go of it. Once at a restaurant, I was trying to get him to cough it up.

"Jeffrey, can Mama have the binky?"

"Nwhhhhh," he said, shaking his head.

We went back and forth a few times, then I gave up. The waitress overheard and came over.

"You're too big to have that binky! Why don't you give it to me," she said.

"Don't you take that binky from my baby!" I said, going on mother-lion autopilot. "If my baby wants his binky, he gets his binky!"

That was me back then. Overprotective and giving conflicting messages. I was on track to raise a very confused mama's boy. So one day, I showed Jeffrey a photo of himself in midjump.

"Jeffrey, who's that big boy?"

"Jeffy."

"Does that big boy need a binky?"

"No."

And he threw it in the sink.

"I'm big boy. No drama, Mama."

I stacked those old hospital pictures in a closet. If Jeffrey wants to look at them one day, he can. But we've got new ones now.

Jeffrey is normal, i.e., a nightmare

Macy's. When my son and I reminisce about our battles, I will tell him about the historic Tantrum at Macy's. The salesclerks still talk about it. There's probably a placard near Clinique, "Sherri Shepherd's son lost his shit here, May 2007."

We were at a mall. Now, to be fair to Jeffrey, he hadn't had his nap yet. But I had a lot of shopping to get done. And to be fair to me, Macy's was having a sale. Not just any old sale, but 50 percent off, plus 10 percent more if you use your Macy's credit card, and another 15 percent if you had a newspaper coupon. That's 75 percent off. In my book, that's free.

We had finished shopping, and I was paying for my clothes. I looked down at my baby boy. He was singing in his stroller. *So far, so good. Let me just put this on my Macy's card and we are home free.* Then, without warning, he arched his back. Every mother knows what that means. That child is going to hurl himself out of the stroller and he doesn't care if he knocks you down in the process. Personally, I think kids have X-Men powers. When they get angry, their bones turn to rubber and they morph into spineless animals that can slide through their stroller straps and onto the floor.

I tried to put him back, but lifting an X-Child is like carrying forty pounds of loose Jell-O. And as soon as I got him in the stroller, he unleashed his reverse mutant power, which was to stiffen his spine so that he was unbendable. Truly like a board. Then he alternated these positions. Loose, stiff, loose, stiff.

All this was accompanied by screams.

"AHHHHHHHHHHH!"

Multiple "my mama beats me" screams that make you want to take him up on it.

I gave him a water bottle.

"Here, Jeffrey, play with this," I said, just wanting to pay and leave. He could sense my desperation. He threw the water bottle.

"Baby, you want to play with a receipt? Look, that's a seven and a four—"

"NOOOOO!"

I gathered my shopping bags and tried to wheel this arching, shrieking lunatic to the parking lot. A few young black women were walking in the store, toward us. I tried to hide behind some T-shirts, but you can't hide a banshee.

They looked around like, "Who's that, doing all that crying?" I thought about how, in the movies, fired cops always turn in their badge and their gun. That's kind of what I wanted to do at that moment. Go to headquarters and surrender my mother card and this child. Put me on desk duty.

The young women spoke to me the way that black women speak to one another—with disapproving glances.

"Another black woman can't control her child," they frowned.

"What am I supposed to do?" I grimaced.

"You are pathetic," they frowned.

"You don't even have kids," I squinted.

"Well, when we do, they sure as hell won't be acting like that," they frowned.

I deserved it, because many years ago, I was one of those childless, know-it-all women. I'd see a child acting up at Target and wonder, *Well, why don't you just do A, B, and C?*

Oh, I could just smack my old self.

Jeffrey was still screaming, so I decided to try the "different tone of voice." (I think that's "E.") I leaned in, close.

"Jeffrey, you got to get it together. Stop it." My voice was loving but stern. *Good job, Sherri,* I told myself. *You did it.*

A little hand flew out of nowhere and hit me in my jaw. After all I did for him! I lost it.

"I . . . you . . . you do not know who you just hit," I told this three-year-old. "You better sit down. Be quiet and sit in this stroller or I'm going to knock you through that wall and right into Lady Foot Locker."

Jeffrey screamed all the way out of the store. But as soon as he was strapped into the car seat, he fell asleep. He just needed a nap. When I tell Jeffrey about the Tantrum at Macy's, I really have to emphasize that I was getting all that stuff for 75 percent off.

Search for my supernanny

Sometimes I look at my son and I can't even believe he's mine. I want to eat him up. I kiss him so much that he pushes me off him.

That's why I had to find the perfect person to take care of him for eight to ten hours a day.

I am a working mom, and a single mom. My ex-husband lives across the country, as does all my family. I can't just drop this kid off at the neighbor's while I go do *The View*. I needed help, and I got it. And if you're a stay-at-home mom who has a problem with that, you will just have to fight me.

Okay, that was my defensive paragraph. I had to get it out of my system, because I know some women judge, "Why you lettin' another woman raise your son?"

The truth is, my nanny is part of the family. Her name is Alejandra, and I kissed a lot of frog nannies before I found her. I didn't know what I wanted; my checklist of qualities to look for was empty, aside from being good with my son.

First there was the Best Friend Nanny. When this woman showed up for the interview, it was like we were separated at birth. We talked alike, we looked alike, we believed the same things, spiritually and culturally. We connected on such a deep level that neither of us noticed that my son had climbed onto the radiator, holding a pair of scissors. Or that he spilled Diet Coke on my white rug.

After she left, I added, "Limited English" to the checklist. I needed someone whose command of my mother tongue was shaky enough to prevent us from talking too much.

Then there was the Hot Latina Nanny. Oh, this one hurt, because she was great with my son. But she had too many things against her. She looked like J.Lo. Remember who else looked like J.Lo? My husband's affair. Hot Latina also wore a thong. I saw it when she gave my son a bath. And not a regular thong, no. This one was jeweled. I thought that was a bit much for a child-care position, especially since I'd graduated to granny panties. Finally, her boobs were huge. Now, my boobs are huge, too, but they are also long, which makes them sweet and nonthreatening. Her boobs were large and *horizontal,* which made them a danger. To put it another way, my boobs were like deer, gently nibbling in a field, and her boobs were like wolves, plotting to devour my family.

If I got a boyfriend (or back together with Jeff), I'd have to fire her by three o'clock. And if my dad came over to visit, I'd have to throw a blanket over her head and have her escorted from the building. After a few days, I told her it wasn't working out. Of course, what I meant was, I am not working out so I can compete with the nanny.

I added "Not Hot" to my checklist.

I met with Arthritic Nanny. She was nice and had lots of experience. Unfortunately, because of her disease, she wouldn't be able to chase Jeffrey without a ten-minute head start. My son would be setting fire to the building's Christmas tree before Arthritic Nanny would have been able to push herself to a standing position.

I added "Nimble" to my checklist.

The Jamaican Nanny had a habit of saying, "I know." We were at the doctor's office. I couldn't find my son, but I did see a flash of yellow darting in and out of various radiation rooms. He was wearing yellow.

"Shouldn't you get him?" I asked.

"I know!" she said.

We'd get into a cab.

"Can you buckle him up?"

"I know!"

She put him in the stroller without securing the straps. He could be out of that chair and on the freeway in less than two seconds.

"Can you strap him in, please?"

"I know!"

We said good-bye and I added "Says 'I'm on it'" to my checklist.

When Alejandra walked into my apartment, I knew she was the one. Spotty English? She's from Colombia. Not Hot? Well, I had to be flexible on that one. Alejandra is hot, but not "hoochie-mama" hot. She's more like "celibate and waiting for the right man" hot. What I'm saying is, the first time she gave Jeffrey a bath, I didn't see jewels. Nimble? Oh yes. Says "I'm on it"? Not sure, see "Spotty English."

All I knew was that she and Jeffrey loved each other, almost immediately. She started speaking to my son in Spanish, and he understood her, because he understood her heart. I could exhale. Finally.

I had thought my ideal nanny was a round white woman, with no face but rosy cheeks. Kinda like Aunt Bea. Alejandra isn't that at all. In fact, she's a Colombian who's converting to Judaism. Yes, you read that right. But she isn't a full Jew yet, so she takes both sets of holidays.

That's cheeky. I like that. Except in December.

Sherri Shepherd's Dad's Daughter

I always tell Jeffrey, "Anything is possible." His life proves that's true. So does mine. I bet yours does, too. He can be anything he wants, but something about Jeffrey tells me that he's going to be a preacher.

Preaching is in his blood. His father's got four relatives who are pastors, mostly in Virginia. They preach out of the Tarpley Baptist Church.

Jeffrey loves to go to church. We go to a six o'clock service in Times Square, and his internal clock chimes every Sunday, at five. "Mama, let me go to church. Want to see Jesus. Praise Him! Hallelujah!"

Of course, he could just be copying me. Maybe that's my dream for him, but he'll grow up to front a punk band, singing "Hallelujah" sarcastically. I know that I'd like to be the pastor's mama. In a Baptist church, the two women held in highest esteem are the First Lady (the pastor's wife) and the First Mother (me, I hope).

The First Mother gets a special seat in the front of the church. Nobody else gets that seat. People come by and pay homage to the First Mother.

Yeah, this isn't about my son. I want that dang seat. I already got my outfit picked out. I'll wear a white suit, and a hat with fruit on it. You got to have fruit on your hat. The more grapes on my head, the closer I feel to Jesus. And I'll have a handkerchief with the initials JM, which stand for "Jeffrey's Mother." Like Sherri Shepherd's Dad, Jeffrey's Mother will sit in her special seat and watch her baby make people feel better.

Like father, like daughter.

> *So write yourself a permission slip to dream big, but keep it to yourself so your kid doesn't think he disappointed you.*

I get ahead of myself

Jeffrey used to fart just like most people do, by letting it rip as the gas built up in his system. Then he figured out how to save his farts. This was huge. Now my son farts on command *and* to a beat. He waits until I come home from work and farts songs, because it makes me laugh. He's my stinky jukebox. He arranges them in a way that would make the conductor of the Boston Pops jealous. The other day, I swear I heard a B-flat.

I can get ahead of myself, as I help this boy grow into a man, and then I miss the fun stuff. My friend said that the first time her son had his heart broken, she held his sobbing body and thought, *I'm going to whup that bitch's ass.* I will want to do the same thing. In fact, with my family history, I'll probably put Jeffrey in the car and take him on a tour of potential neighborhoods. "Show me that bitch's building! Your mama will take it from here!"

I worry about that day when he becomes someone else's. When another woman comes before me in his heart. After I've held him so close, will I be able to let him go? When a father walks his daughter down the aisle, he's releasing her into another man's care. It's symbolic of a shift. How am I going to release my little man to another?

I'm already praying for his wife, because I'll be unable to shut up.

"Jeffrey likes his shirts to be hung *this* way. He always liked his shirts like that, since he was a baby."

I want Jeffrey to be a mama's boy while he's growing up, and a man's man once he gets there. But mostly, I want to have a good relationship with my daughter-in-law so she'll let me see my grandbabies.

Grandbabies. Daughter-in-law. Good Lord, he's three.

So write yourself a permission slip to live in the moment, because kids don't fart on command forever. (Okay, the boys do. But you know what I mean.)

About the Author

Whether on stage or screen, comedienne/actress Sherri Shepherd never fails to delight audiences with her magnetic personality and hilarious sense of humor, which is showcased in her position as co-host of ABC's Emmy-nominated *The View*. Sherri will also star in her new Lifetime series, *Sherri*. The show, in which she also serves as co-executive producer, is loosely based on her life and stand-up comedy, and will premiere in fall 2009.

A self-described "class clown," Sherri always wanted to pursue a performing career. She relocated to Los Angeles during high school and considered being a mortician but opted for a job as a legal secretary instead. In 1990 she came face-to-face with destiny. After witnessing Andrew Dice Clay on stage, Sherri was egged on by her friends to put together her own act. Her love for performing was instantaneous; success, however, was not. For five years, Sherri toiled as a secretary by day and hopped on the bus at night to go do her stand-up. She finally got her first real break with the comedy series *Cleghorne!* starring former *Saturday Night Live* alum Ellen Cleghorne.

She's been fortunate enough to work steadily while fine-tuning her craft through comedy, scene-study, and improvisational work-shops. As an accomplished stand-up comic, she has performed at The Comedy Store, The Improv, and Laugh Factory in Hollywood. Sherri also has her own comedy DVD, titled *No Refund, No Exchange*.

Not one to rest on her laurels, Sherri will continue to reprise her hysterical role as Angie Jordan, wife to Tracy Morgan's character on the Emmy-winning *30 Rock*. In November 2009, Sherri will be seen in the upcoming feature film *Precious*, alongside Mo'Nique and Mariah Carey, directed by Lee Daniels (*Monsters Ball*). Sherri most recently co-starred in the Dreamworks hit feature *Madagascar: Escape 2 Africa*, where she voiced the character of Ben Stiller's mother. She also serves as a national spokesperson for the *March of Dimes*.

Sherri has been on the couch of many talk shows, such as *The Tonight Show with Jay Leno*, *Jimmy Kimmel*, and *The Bonnie Hunt Show*, and she holds the record for being the most-booked guest on *The Ellen Show* (twenty-three times). She can also be seen as Sgt. Judy, Robert Barone's partner, in *Everybody Loves Raymond*. Her film roles include co-starring alongside Queen Latifah in *Beauty Shop* and Ashton Kutcher in *Guess Who*.

Sherri's greatest accomplishment, however, is being the proud mother of her four-year-old son, Jeffrey Charles, Jr. Away from the set, she enjoys karaoke, skating, church activities, and a good game of Taboo.